ADULT JOKE BOOK FOR MEN

(And Very Tolerant Women)

Team Golfwell

Team Golfwell

ADULT JOKE BOOK FOR MEN, (And Very Tolerant Women), Copyright © 2021, Team Golfwell as to the collective work only. All rights reserved. No part of this book may be reproduced or transmitted in any form or by any means, electronic or mechanical, including photocopying, recording, or by any information storage and retrieval system, without written permission from the author, except for brief quotations as would be used in a review.

This is a work of fiction, and nothing is to be taken seriously.

ADULTS ONLY PLEASE

ISBN: 9798526902373 (Amazon Paperback)

ISBN: 9781991161659 (Ingram Paperback)

ISBN: 9781991161666 (Ingram EPUB)

Contents

Advertising 1

Airline Fun 8

Alcohol 13

Anger 26

Bad Jokes: (Some Are Funny) 29

Bad People 44

Barber Shop 47

Battle of the Sexes 49

Big Butts 57

Brainy Humor 59

Business 65

Cannibals and Comedians 67

Cars 69

Chinese 74

Consultants 77

Courtship	80
Criticism	96
Dark Humor	101
Desert Island	108
Doctors	110
Employment	120
Engineers	123
Entitlement	128
Epitaphs	129
Ethnic Humor	131
Excuses	138
Failure	140
Family	144
Farmers	147
Fast Thinking	150
Father's Day	153

Fitness	154
Gambling	155
Genius	157
Getting Even	160
Golf	162
Golf Rules	167
Heaven	171
Horses	180
Hospitals	181
Insanity	182
Irony	184
Judo	186
Jumping to Conclusions	188
Lawyers	190
Live in the Moment	197
Marital Bliss	197

Masturbation 222

Mathematics 223

Men 225

Mental Health Facility 227

Neighbors 227

New Yorkers 229

News Media 230

No Respect 231

Payback 231

Octopus 233

Optimism 234

Penguins 235

Pessimists 236

Pilots 237

Play on Words 238

Politics 243

Porn 249

Poverty 249

Practical 250

Prescriptions 252

Priests and Preachers 253

Private Parts 256

Problems 258

Procrastination 258

Reincarnation 260

Religion 262

Research 264

Riddles 265

Romantic 266

Salespersons 268

Santa Claus 270

School Fun 271

Self-Help	273
Senior Fun	276
Shopping	288
Sign Language	288
Society in Decline	291
Stupidity	292
Tech	302
Too Many Lawsuits	304
UFC	305
Walked Into a Bar	306
Women	308
World	310
Thank you	311
We Want to Hear From You	312

Advertising

"The best ideas come as jokes."

- David Ogilvy, Advertising Tycoon and better known as the Father of Advertising"

* Here's a toast to the insane ones, the Admen! They are misfits. They are rebels. They are all troublemakers.

They don't see things the way most people do. And they don't like rules. They don't like the way things are presently and you must keep aware of them since they change things.

Some say they are absolutely crazy but there is a genius to them since they are insane enough to sincerely believe they can influence the world, and without knowing any better they change the world.

- Rob Siltanen

* "I'm thinking of starting a liquor brand and getting free advertising from the other major brands."

"That's probably not going to happen," his friend replied.

"I'm going to call it "Responsibly."

* A college advertising lecture is taking place. The lecturer is showing the class his anti-drug TV Commercial Public Service Announcement and says, "I have written a simple, yet effective campaign against drug use." And then he holds up a poster he designed.

The poster shows two circles, one big and the other small. The big one is titled, "This Is Your Brain" and the small hole is titled, "This Is Your Brain on Drugs." The lecturer continues and says, "Areas in which my campaign was used had a reduction of drug use of up to 10% over the first campaign month."

A student rises and says, "I can do better."

The lecturer says, "Well, I'll give you time to make your campaign, and if you can beat my campaign, I'll give you an A for this course.

The next week the student comes into class with a poster and the local police chief. The chief says, "This young man created an anti-drug campaign that decreased drug use in our area by over 50%."

The lecturer asks, "Really? Let's see it."

The police chief confirms the campaign's effectiveness, and the student holds up a similar poster with two circles, one small and the other big. The first one is titled 'This Is Your Butthole." The other is titled, "This Is Your Butthole After You Get Jailed for Drugs."

* False Advertising. An accountant, on his own, walked along the beaches of the French Riviera for the first time. He'd been working very hard and planned this vacation for some time.

A bit lonely, he sat on his beach towel wearing dark wraparound sunglasses and watched the girls on the beach. He noticed a Frenchman, just about the same age as him walking the beach and being followed by five gorgeous women, all bare-breasted, slowly following the man.

The Frenchman walked by the accountant on his way to the refreshment stand and the accountant had to interrupt him. The beautiful women stood by at a distance.

"Monsieur, I need to speak with you?"

"Oui, what eez on your mind?" said the Frenchman.

"Excusez-moi, but I couldn't help but notice the beautiful women following you along the beach and wondered how you do it?" The accountant asked.

"Monsieur, do you know the secret technique?"

"What secret?" asked the accountant.

"Well, before you take zee walk on zee beach, you place zee potato in zee swimsuit," said the Frenchman.

"Oooh, I see! Yes, I see," said the accountant.

So, the accountant rushed off to the market and bought a big potato and came back to the beach and walked for hours up and down the beach, but absolutely no women were following him.

He couldn't figure it out! Then he noticed the French guy and jogged up to him.

"Listen, I've got a potato and put it in my swimsuit, and I've been walking up and down this beach for hours and no women follow me? They don't even notice me?" said the accountant.

The Frenchman paused and looked the accountant up and down. "Monsieur, you place zee potato in zee front of the swimsuit."

* I dislike the concept of advertising since it is lucrative and winds up attracting very bright and creative young minds. The rest of the creative people who choose art are not as creative or clever, in my opinion.

- Banksy

* I got an advertising email. It said it knows how to spell Google maps backwards. I thought, that's just spam.

* A burnt out advertising executive decides he has had enough of the rat race & buys a property way out in the desert. No electricity, no phones - no company. He has read everything he can and after a few weeks is getting a bit bored.

One afternoon he sees dust cloud rising way in the distance coming towards him, a while later a crusty old man gets out of a battered old and puts out his hand.

"Hello friend, I'm your closest neighbor, live about 20 miles up the road, thought we'd hold a party to welcome you to the area."

"Sounds great" says the ad-man.

"I hear you city boys like your drugs and drink so we'll get that in for ya."

"Sounds awesome!" says the ad-man.

"We tend to get a bit drunk and horny 'round here after all those drugs & drink though, can ya handle yerself if a bit of sex is on the cards?"

"Fantastic!" says the ad-man. "This all sounds great, what time should I come and what should I wear?"

"Doesn't really matter," says the old man. "It is only going to be you and me…"

* A man goes to a carnival advertising the three greatest samurai on earth and as he enters the tent he the expectant crowd eager to get their money's worth.

The ringmaster announces, "The third greatest samurai!" The samurai steps up. A box is opened and a fly buzzes out. He draws his sword, there's a flash of light, and the fly falls in two equal halves. The crowd cheers.

"The second greatest samurai!" the ringmaster announces. Another samurai steps up. Another fly is released. A flash of the blade, and the fly drops beheaded. The crowd grows wild.

Finally, the ringmaster screams, "And now, the one, the only, the greatest samurai who ever lived!" The crowd grows completely still waiting for action. The fly is released. The blade flashes... and the fly continues to buzz around.

"Ladies and Gentlemen," says the announcer, "the fly lives... but will never be a father."

Airline Fun

* An airline is a requirement. No matter how much land there is, you can't be a real country unless you manufacture a beer and have an airline. The country might have a sports team, or nuclear weapons, and that all helps it to become recognized as a country. But the main ingredients for being recognized as a country are a beer made in the country and an airline.

- Frank Zappa

* An international flight from Asia to the US was carrying 198 passengers but the crew, unfortunately, discovered an hour into the flight there were only 40 meals on the plane.

After trying to figure out what to do, the Flight Crew came up with a solution. They advised the passengers, "We apologize to you, and we are still trying to figure out how this occurred, but we have only 40 dinners on board, and we need to feed all 198 of you on this flight."

A loud muttering and moaning started amongst the passengers. The chief flight attendant continued to try and quiet everyone down, "Anyone who is kind enough to give up their dinner so someone else could eat, will receive unlimited free alcoholic beverages during the entire duration of the flight."

A second announcement was made two hours later, "If anyone wants to change their mind, we still have 40 dinners available."

* What's the small difference between a Captain of an airliner and God?

A. God doesn't think He's a captain of an airliner.

* When I hear the pilots address the passengers over the intercom, they seem to refer to passengers as "folks"? Why do they do that? I don't like that. It would be nice to have addressed us as something else other than suggesting we are part of the unwashed masses.

- C.E. Murphy,

* The airline employee finally rushed back to the departure desk after checking for an available seat for a customer.

"Your best bet is to Apparate." She told the customer.

"Excuse me, what is that?" Said the customer.

"Sorry, that's just a little Harry Potter humor."

(In the wizarding world, to Apparate means to appear at your intended destination at will. This method of travel is used by wizards and witches.)

- Anecdote from Rainbow Rowell, American Author

* A 777 was coming into New York JFK after a long-haul trip from Frankfurt. The captain looking forward to a break, announced over the intercom, "Ladies and gentlemen we are now making our final approach into JFK, we hope you've enjoyed flying with us and we'll see you again soon, and we hope you have a safe onward journey to your final destination."

Inadvertently leaving the intercom on, he turned to his co-pilot and said, "Well what's up for you this evening?"

"Oh, my wife is at the hotel, Joe, and she's got seats booked for theatre, I don't know which one, what plans do you have?"

The passengers enjoyed hearing this exchange between the pilots.

The captain continued. "Hey, my divorce was finalized last week so I'll be taking a long soak in the bath before ordering dinner in my room. I'm thinking I'll call the pretty new blonde stewardess, Josephine, I think her name is, and take her out for a drink then take her back to my room and give her a good rogering."

The passengers began to cheer, as Josephine scrambled to turn off the intercom and ran up the aisle. She tripped over an old lady's carryon bag halfway up and fell flat on her face.

The old lady said, "There's no need to hurry my dear, he's got to take a bath first."

* A 4-seater Cessna 172 crashed into a cemetery early this afternoon near Warsaw and the Polish search and rescue workers recovered 200 bodies. The number is expected to climb as digging continues into the evening.

* A teetotaler sat next to an Irish man on a long-distance flight out of Sydney.

After the plane reached altitude, the drink cart was taken out and the flight attendant began going back and forth taking drink orders. The Irishman ordered an Irish whiskey and a pint of Gat which were brought to him.

The flight attendant asked the teetotaler if he cared to have a drink. He replied in disgust, "I haven't touched a drink in my life, I'd rather be savagely attacked by a dozen wild women than allow any rotgut alcohol to enter my body."

The Irishman handed his drink back to the to the flight attendant and said, "That's class! I'll take the women! That's a great choice, Begorrah!"

* After detailed scientific research, use of the Hubbell space telescope, and further years of research, a NASA Administration scientific study has proved and concluded the mysterious rings of Saturn are made up of lost airline luggage.

- Mark Russell

Alcohol

* As I poured myself a drink, I wondered why people drink if something bad happens? And why do people drink to celebrate when something good happens?

Me? Oh, I drink if nothing is happening in order to make something happen.

- Charles Bukowski

* Joe was traveling through the Florida Everglades and stopped at a little bar. He walked in and noticed an old sign hanging by the bar:

"IF YOU CAN PASS THE TEST, FREE BEER AND WINE FOR A YEAR."

Joe scratched his head and asked the proprietor, "Sir, what is… 'The Test'"?

The proprietor looked at Joe and shook his head. "You don't want to know."

"Yes, I do," said Joe.

"You really want to know?"

"Yeah, just curious. I like beer and wine especially free beer and wine," Joe replied.

The proprietor says, "Well, here's how it goes. You drink that gallon bottle of Prairie Fire."

"What's Prairie Fire?" Joe asked.

"Tabasco Sauce and Vodka. You got to drink the whole thing down all at once – no stoppin' and you can't grimace one bit. Next, there's a gator back there with a sore tooth - the proprietor points out the window. You gotta pull that tooth out with your bare hands. Third, there's a lady upstairs getting on in her years and she's never had a climax. You gotta make things right for her – you know what I'm talking about?"

Joe sits there shaking his head. "As much as I'd like free beer, that's crazy. You know I've done some crazy things but that's ridiculous."

Well, Joe drinks a few, then sits up and says, "Wherez that Plaree-e-e P-h-lire?" Then Joe grabs the gallon jug and chugs it all down. His face is redder than the rising sun, tears are streaming down his face. He slams the empty gallon bottle down on the bar and staggers out back.

The others at the bar hear hair-raising grunts and loud roars. They look out the window at the pen outside and see the huge alligator struggling to get away while Joe is dragging it back into the pen. There's a huge roar then eerie silence.

Joe staggered out with his shirt and pants ripped to shreds. He's bleeding from scratches and cuts all over his body as he walked slowly back into the bar.

"Okay," Joe says, "Where's that lady who's got the sore tooth?"

* I don't believe in promoting alcohol, mayhem, murder, or any criminal behavior, or drugs. I sincerely believe no one should ever engage in such activities. However, they've worked for me very well in past years.

- Hunter S. Thompson, author of "Hell's Angels, A Strange and Terrible Saga"

* I feel sorry for people who don't imbibe. Everyone needs a good stiff drink now and then. Teetotalers groggily wake up in the morning, and it's sad to think they aren't going to feel any better than that all day.

- Dean Martin

* I spent tons of money, on liquor, fast women, and fast motorcycles.

The rest of my money, I just spent in a reckless and wasteful manner.

- Anon.

* I got wasted at my sister's wedding. I won the dance contest, caught the bouquet, caught the

garter, got engaged, and got into a fight as I crossed the dance floor just trying to get another drink.

- Anon.

* A man stood outside his house after a bitter divorce and noticed a crate of beer bottles. He angrily looked down at the crate and took out an empty bottle and smashed against the wall shouting, "You are the reason I don't have a wife!"

He picked up a second bottle and smashed it against the wall shouting, "You are the reason I don't have children!"

He picked up a third bottle, and smashed it against the wall shouting, "You are the reason I don't have a job."

He picked up the fourth bottle. It was a perfectly good bottle of beer with the cap still on it. He said to the bottle, "YOU STAND ASIDE, I KNOW YOU WERE NOT INVOLVED!"

* Whiskey doesn't solve problems. Then again, neither does a glass of water.

* I don't get inebriated. I just have less class and a lot more fun.

* I'll drink to that! Then again, honestly, I'll drink to almost anything.

* Tough guys can't dance? Oh yeah? Trust me. You can dance.

- Tequila

* An old man named Frank passed away and his wishes were to have his ashes scattered in the sea off the coast of California.

Frank loved to drink Scotch and directed in his will when his ashes were scattered, every adult in the boat would have a glass of his favorite Scotch and would toast in his honor as his ashes were scattered in the sea.

The wind was strong on his funeral day, and the boat carrying his ashes and loved ones rocked back and forth. One of his friends even became seasick it was so rough.

When it came time to scatter his ashes, glasses of his favorite scotch were raised, but when the good Reverend tossed his ashes into the sea, the ashes were blown by the strong wind into most of the raised scotch glasses.

The mourners grimaced at the ashes floating on the top of their scotch.

One of them broke the silence by saying, "Frank's still drinking his favorite scotch!"

* A good girlfriend will stop you from drinking when you've had too much. Your best friend forever will say, "Bitch, you better drink this 'cause we're not wasting this sh*t."

* A tough looking woman walked into the clubhouse bar and looked around. Filthy, smelly, and wearing ragged clothes, she pounded her fist on the bar, and raised her arm up in the air exposing her hairy armpit, and shouted, "Who's going to buy me a f*ckin' drink!"

No one in the bar responded. Everyone was trying to ignore her as the club bartender walked over to tell her to leave.

All at once, old Harry in the back of the bar called out in his cracking feeble voice, "I'll buy that acrobat a drink."

"Pour me a shot of whiskey!" The tough woman said as she pounded her fist on the bar.

The bartender knew old Harry was good for it, so he poured her a shot and she downed it in one gulp.

She pounded the shot glass back on the bar and raised her arm again and said, "Who's gonna buy me another f*ckin' drink!"

"I'll buy that acrobat another one," said Harry.

The bartender looked up at Harry and said, "Harry, What the hell? Why do you think this woman's an acrobat?"

"She's got to be an acrobat, since I haven't seen a woman raise her leg so high in my life!"

* Did I ever knock a horse out? Yes, I must tell you that is true. I did knock a horse out with only a single punch. I was at a fiesta at my mother's, and someone wagered a nice bottle of scotch if I could do it.

- Roberto Duran

* There should be a truck which drives around the business district at 5 pm as workers go to catch the train home playing bagpipe music so men could come out to the curb and greet it with dollars in their hands, just like an ice cream truck, but only with, you guessed it, scotch and fine cigars.

* A new member at an exclusive golf club finished his golf round and walked into the clubhouse bar. He noticed a friend he hadn't seen in months seated in the corner. He went over and sat with him for a while.

Then the new member walked over to the bar and sat down and ordered another drink for himself and introduced himself to the bartender. After talking with the bartender for a while, the guy said, "Are you a betting man?"

"Not usually, but occasionally," said the bartender.

The guy smiled, "I'd like to know if you will enter into a wage of say $50 that I can munch on my right eye."

The bartender laughed, wondering if this guy had a screw loose, and said, "I'll take that bet."

The new guy surprised the bartender by showing him he had a glass eye. He put his glass eye in his mouth like it was a marble and bit it.

"That's not fair," said the bartender, "I didn't know you had a glass eye?"

"Okay, okay. I'll bet you $50 I can munch on my other eye."

The bartender figured this guy can't have two glass eyes and agreed to take the bet.

Slowly, the man pulls out his set of false teeth and uses them to munch on his eye.

"Sh*t!" said the bartender who is now pissed off and hands over $50.

The guy starts drinking whiskey shots with beer chasers and gets hammered.

"I'm sorry, that really wasn't fair. How about another bet."

The bartender listens.

The guy continued, "I'll bet you $500 that I can stand on this swivel chair and piss into 15 shot glashes and not piss a drop on your bar – yesh shur, I'll fill those 15 shot glashes and you can place those shot glashes anyway you f#cking want on the bar."

The bartender smiled and took the bet. He scattered 15 shot glasses over on the bar - two of the shot glasses were 10 feet away from the swivel chair.

The guy shakily climbs and stands on the swivel chair. He's teetering back and forth while he pulls out his penis and then urinates all over the bar missing every single shot glass!

The bartender is laughing his head off. He's jumping up and down shouting, "I knew you'd miss!" Then the bartender happily cleared the shot glasses off the bar and started cleaning the bar with a sponge and bucket as the man hands over $500 to the bartender.

The bartender looked at the guy with pity and said, "You've got to be nuts thinking you'd be able to do that?"

"Oh, not too nuts, since I bet the guy in the corner $2,000 I'd stand on the seat, piss all over your bar, and you'd laugh and clean it up."

* Whisky and I are not a good combination. One disappears and the other ends up naked.

- Anon.

* Joe is late for his usual Sunday tee time. The course is crowded, and Joe can't find a place to park. He searched and searched going up and down the parking lot but couldn't find a spot. He began to pray.

"Please Lord, if you help me find a parking spot right now, I promise to go to church every Sunday and never drink alcohol again!"

A moment later, he sees a beautiful empty spot right next to the pro shop.

"Never mind. Found one!"

* A man and his wife finished playing a round of golf and were sitting in the bar, having a few

drinks. After the drinks, they got in their car and were driving home, when a cop stopped the couple and began writing the husband a ticket for not wearing his seatbelt.

The man became quite upset and denied the accusation. He told the officer, "You're a blind asshole! You're just looking to write a ticket. Do you need your quota of tickets for the day?"

The man continued non-stop, "You couldn't have seen me not wearing my seatbelt, just ask my wife! She saw me buckle-up and she's an eye-witness to the fact I was wearing my seat belt."

The officer asked the wife, and she replied, "Well I got to say, 'yes' since I never argue with my husband after he's been drinking."

    * "Happiness is three things. First, a nice, rare filet mignon steak, second, a bottle of fine whiskey, and third, a great dog to eat the rare steak."

    - Johnny Carson

Anger

* "Hello, Harry," said George wondering about him. "We thought we might have heard you say something in your soft and soothing tones? We're glad you don't keep your anger inside you – you shouldn't bottle anger. It's good you let it all out even more than you do since there still might be a few people several hundred kilometers away who didn't hear you yet."

- J.K. Rowling

* You can tell a lot about a woman by her hands. For example, if they are placed around your neck she is probably slightly upset.

* It isn't good to try and argue with an angry idiot. He'll beat you down to his low level and win with all his experience.

* Whenever you get angry don't move, just stand there, and start counting back from 10 to 1 out

loud. Throw a punch at 3 since you'll usually catch him off guard.

* Whenever I begin a sentence with 'No offense' it means I'm about to insult you but don't get angry.

* Be very careful with angry words. You can later apologize for saying the words, but you can't make them forgotten.

* The extreme anger I have for you has been inside me for years continuing to hurt deeply inside me even though what you did to me never bothered you. My telling you this now is my revenge on you… Uh, I think?

* <u>An Angry Man's Toast</u>:

"Here's to you,

"Here's to me,

"The best of friends we'll always be,

"But if by chance we disagree,

"Then go f#ck yourself and here's to me."

* "There's no point in getting angry if you can't turn into the Hulk."

- Anon.

* "It's very important not to go to bed angry in a relationship. You should stay up and fight."

- Phyllis Diller

* There are some the things that intelligent men fear the most: an angry sea in a storm, a dark night with no moon, and (the most feared) the anger of a gentleman."

- Patrick Rothfuss

Bad Jokes: (Some Are Funny)

* Caution. Grim humor. Joe went on a solo safari into the heart of Africa. He found himself lost just as his satellite phone battery ran out. He knew it would be dark soon and very dangerous to try and travel during the night.

Joe decided to find somewhere safe. He looked for a place where rescuers could find him, and he needed water. So, he decided on camping near a river.

He luckily found a riverbank with a large sheltering tree on the bank. After he sat under the tree a while, he noticed an enormous lion walking towards him.

He tried to run the other way but saw a ferocious leopard approaching from the other side. So, he climbed the tree.

As he climbed up, he saw a giant boa constrictor wrapped around a large branch beginning to slither down toward him.

He quickly climbed down the tree and sat at the foot of the tree and began to say his final prayers. He realized this was the end, so he took out his harmonica and began to play a final tune which sounded like the Beatles song, "Hey Jude," only at a slow sorrowful pace.

Soon his sad and haunting music filled the area. He looked up and noticed the lion had stopped approaching and stood still except for movement in its tail which swung in cadence to the tune.

He looked at the leopard who was now resting on the ground moving his head in cadence to the music.

He looked up and saw the snake coiled around a branch, with its eyes closed and its tongue flicking in and out in cadence to the tune.

Joe was amazed. He felt great respect for all the animals and reaffirmed his belief that music is indeed a universal language soothing even to the most savage.

He played on in total peace with the animals.

Just then a giant crocodile quickly rose out of the river and, "SNAP!" The giant croc bit Joe's head off!

The lion, the leopard, and the snake turned to the crocodile and asked, "Why the hell did you do that? We were enjoying his wonderful music!"

"Please speak up," said the croc. "My hearing aid's broken!"

* A frustrated woman waiting in a long waiting line at the checkout, wanted to buy just a bag of dog food when an annoying guy behind her said, "Oh, so you have a dog?"

The woman was further annoyed by the obvious silly question, and sarcastically answered, "No, it's for me. I'm going back on the "dog food diet." I keep a handful of kibbles in my pocket, and every time I get hungry, I just eat a few instead of snacking on unhealthy food."

"Oh, really," said the annoying guy behind her?

She continued, "I heard dog food was nutritionally complete, so it works out well for me. My doctor told me I had to quit after I lost twenty pounds. Oh, and I've lost 10 lbs. already and I want to lose that last ten so I'm eating dog food despite the side effects."

"Really, did it poison you," asked the guy? He was getting disgusted with the thought of eating dog food but was still fascinated.

"No," she said. "The dog food is great, but after I lost the first 10 lbs. I almost got hit by a car when I was crossing the street to sniff a terrier's ass."

* Joe sat down in a bar and ordered a beer. After a couple of minutes, he heard a small voice... "Hi!"

Joe looked around, confused, then realized the voice came out of the bowl of peanuts in front of him on the counter. Joe tried to get a peanut. Then he heard, "I just want to say you look really nice tonight, Joe. That haircut suits you and your shirt is a great color. Very smart."

Joe is stunned. He reeled away from the bar thinking he must be losing his mind. He decided he needed fresh air, so he headed for the back door.

Right by the back door was a cigarette machine. Joe decided a cigarette might help calm his nerves.

As he approached the machine he heard an angry voice. "What the hell you lookin' at? Hey you! You're a pussy. You're a noodle – a weak and ugly bastard! F*ck off!"

The bartender noticed all of this and said, "Oh, sorry about that sir. The peanuts are always complimentary. That smoke machine has been and still is… out of order."

* A man who lived in Texas and drove trains for a living. He loved his job. He loved to make the train begin slowly then accelerate the train to extreme speeds.

Unfortunately, one day he was going too fast and crashed. He survived but a passenger was killed. He was arrested for reckless homicide and was found guilty and sentenced to death.

When the day of the execution came, he requested a single apple as his last meal. After eating the apple, he was put into the electric chair. The switch was turned on, sparks flew, smoke filled the air - but nothing happened. The man was perfectly fine.

Under a little-known Texan Special law, a failed execution was considered Divine Intervention, and the man was set free, and he got his old job back driving a train. Still reckless, he crashed again, this time killing two people.

Again, he was sentenced to death, and for his final meal, he requested two apples. After eating two apples, he was put into the electric chair. The current was turned on, yet he was still unbelievably not harmed!

He again got his old job back, crashed again, killed three people, found guilty and sentenced to death. On the day of his execution, he requested his final meal: three apples.

"No," said the executioner. "I've had it with you and your apples and walking out of here alive. I'm not giving you a thing to eat. We're strapping you in and doing this now."

The man was strapped into the electric chair without a last meal. Incredibly, again the man was not harmed! The executioner was speechless.

The man looked at the executioner and said, "Oh, the apples had nothing to do with it. I'm just a bad conductor."

* A pair of booster car battery cables walk into a bar. The bartender said, "Okay, I'm a bit reluctant, but I'll serve you, as long as you two don't start anything."

* King Arthur walked into the meeting room to see his famous "Round Table" for the first time. He was amazed with the craftmanship, and asked, "Who was the fine woodworker who built this fine round table for my worthy knights and I?"

Sir Lancelot said, "Your majesty, this round table was built by a knight."

"And what knight is that" asked the King?

"Why none other than, Sir Cumpherence."

* A blonde woman construction worker was working a few floors above the ground and accidentally cut her ear off. She yelled down to the street. "Hey, you! Sir! I just cut my ear off, can you pick it up for me?"

The man saw the ear lying on the ground and picked it up. "Is this it?"

"No," said the blonde. "Mine had a pencil behind it."

* Two baby fish are swimming and just having fun loving every minute of being alive. A larger fish was amused seeing the two of them just simply enjoying themselves and having fun and swam next to them. The larger fish said to the baby fish, "Morning boys, you two are having a lot of fun! How's the water?"

The baby fish didn't respond and followed the big fish in silence until the first one turned to the other and asked, "What the hell is water?"

* Girls can usually tell when I like them since I blush or start telling bad jokes.

- Zac Efron, American Actor

* A poor woman who couldn't afford to raise children gave birth to twin boys and gave them up for adoption.

A wealthy Mexican family adopted one boy and named him "Juan." An Egyptian family adopted the other and named him "Amal."

Many years pass, and Juan sent a picture of himself to the woman who is now married. She showed the picture to her husband and said, "Look at this picture, it's my son, Juan! I haven't seen him in twenty years! Let's go see him and my other son in Egypt."

Her husband is taken aback. Then he said, "But your sons are twins. If you've seen Juan, you've seen Amal."

* I find a lot of enjoyment when I come across a bad joke, and I love telling a bad joke now and then. I enjoy letting others know there's going to be a very bad joke about to come out of my mouth.

- Andy Kindler, American Comedian

* A large roast beef sandwich followed by a plate of French fries walked into a bar. The bartender looked at them and said, "Sorry, we don't serve food."

* A blonde took her first flight on an airplane and was extremely excited. As soon as she boarded the plane, a Boeing 787, she began jumping up and down in excitement, while running up and down the aisle shouting, "BOEING! BOEING!! BOEING! BO --"

The annoyed captain heard the shouting and interrupted her and said, "Be silent!"

Everyone on the plane stopped what they were doing and stared at the captain. The excited blonde paused then she politely nodded an "Aye, aye, Captain" and began shouting, "OEING! OEING! OEING! OE...."

* A man was in a terrible accident and lost his left arm and left leg. He's all right now.

* A rutabaga and a banana are in a boat. The rutabaga became bored with the boat ride, so the rutabaga started rocking the boat.

The banana got annoyed and told the rutabaga to stop. So, the rutabaga stopped rocking.

A few minutes later, the rutabaga again became bored and began rocking the boat. The banana became angry and told the rutabaga to stop rocking the boat. So, the rutabaga stopped.

Ten minutes later, the rutabaga laughed at the banana and said, "Hey this if fun!" And again, the rutabaga started rocking the boat.

The banana got pissed off and said, "Hey! Don't rock this f*cking boat or I'm going to throw your ass out of this boat!" The rutabaga stopped.

Ten minutes later, the rutabaga was at it again and the banana pushed the rutabaga off the boat!

* A young man was in love and proposed to his girlfriend and gave her an engagement ring right before he went into the army.

After he was discharged, his future bride told him her mother had become an invalid who needed her 24/7. She still loved him very much but didn't want to ruin his life.

He told her to keep the ring and he understood her situation, but they decided once a year to meet at a nearby lake on the dock where he first proposed to her.

So, every year they met on the dock until as the years passed, the man developed Alzheimer's and went to the wrong dock for their annual meeting. He waited and waited and decided to fish while he was waiting.

Meanwhile, his beloved is on the right dock but after waiting and waiting, she gave up and tossed the engagement ring into the lake thinking he did not love her anymore and left.

The old gentleman was still fishing on the wrong dock but suddenly felt a tug on his line. He reeled it in slowly and to his amazement, he caught…a rutabaga.

 * As you may know, Carlos Castaneda was a brilliant Peruvian writer and a mystic who wrote and practiced Shamanism. His well-known book, "The Teachings of Don Juan," sold millions of copies and was translated into 17 languages.

Carlos did not wear shoes as he loved to connect with the earth, so his feet were heavily calloused. He ate very little and was a frail man.

Because of his mystical beliefs, he had a diet with lots of raw vegetables, such as raw onions, and garlic, and he was known to have very bad breath.

So, the one word that best characterizes Carlos Castaneda, the brilliant writer and Ph.D. could be supercallousedfragilemysticwithextrahalitosis.

* Caution. They may not get any worse than this next one. Very sorry.

Now, a little while ago, I was in a long line for a new video game and stood behind a beautiful girl. The line was so long, I started up a conversation with her and as we talked, things went very well so I asked her out for a movie that evening.

I picked her up and off we went to the movie. We didn't book tickets online and since the movie had just come out, there was a long line and only one ticket seller. But the long line gave us more time to learn more about each other which was good.

After we got our tickets, the theater was still emptying out from the prior showing, so we had to wait again in a long line which gave us more time to talk. We talked about everything, our friends, our family. It was great.

When the people quit coming out of the prior show, an army of cleaners went in, so we had more time to talk in the long line of people waiting to take their seats.

After 15 minutes, we finally got in and as we sat down, the girl said she was terribly thirsty, so I went and got a drink for her. Seemed like everyone else had the same idea, and again there was a long line for drinks. I entertained myself thinking about what to do after the movie with my new girl.

Finally, I got the drinks and headed back to our seats. I gave a drink to her, then realized I needed to go to the bathroom and told her I'd be right back. I'd missed the opening of the movie anyway, so I didn't mind leaving but when I got to the bathroom, there was a huge line with only one toilet and one urinal in the whole theater. I had no choice but to wait in line. I didn't get annoyed since I felt bad for the people who were behind me way back in the line which was forming fast due to only one urinal and one toilet.

Eventually, I made it back and settled in to watch the film and the film was very good even though I now missed over half of it. She was enjoying it and that made me feel very good to see her enjoying it.

After the film, she wanted to go to one of the little restaurants outside the theater. I agreed, but again, it seemed like everyone else had the same idea and we waited quite a bit in the long line for a table. We must have been in line for nearly an hour but that was fine since we talked and talked and were getting along just fine, telling jokes, and learning about each other's interests and hobbies.

The waitress apologized after we were seated and took our orders. We ended up enjoying a lot of food as the waiting in line increased our appetites and we also drank too many glasses of wine and both of us were feeling a little rocky.

She was still having fun, so I asked her if she wanted to go to one of the clubs in town and she agreed. We didn't want to drive since we drank a bit too much, so I told her we'd better take a taxi and unbelievably, there was a huge line for taxis at the taxi stand. I didn't think there would be a demand for taxis as it wasn't raining but we talked about all the skyscraper buildings lit up at night. After a long wait, (the taxis showed up one by one) we finally got into a taxi and headed to the club.

When we got to the club, there was a huge line of people waiting to get in but to my amazement, this beautiful girl is still having a great time even though we were in another long line again. We talked effortlessly, and I knew this was going to be the start of a great relationship.

When we finally got into the club, we started dancing for a while, then took a booth. She told me she was thirsty, so I got up and went to the bar and again there was a huge line for drinks with only one bartender. She told me she liked to drink punch, so, I asked the guy in front of me if there was any other place in the club I could get a non-alcoholic drink like a punch.

He turned to me and said, "No, sorry man. There is no punch line."

Bad People

* In this world, there is a hole – a huge black and dark pit. This huge black and dark pit is filled with bad people who are filled with sh*t.

- Stephen Sondheim, from "Sweeny Todd"

* People shouldn't be divided into two categories with one category for wicked people and the other for noble people.

The world is full of a variety of people who have both good and bad qualities. The good and bad qualities in each person are all mixed with a salad dressing coating of both the good and bad causing confusion and conflict.

- Lemony Snicket

* Los Angeles police had 5 men in a line up for a witness to identify a robbery suspect. One of the suspects in the lineup just had to correct the detective when he was asked to repeat the words, "Give me your money or I'll shoot." He told the detective, "No, I didn't say it that way."

* A Michigan defendant was on trial for Drug Possession, and he raised the defense of being searched without a warrant. The prosecutor argued that the officers had reasonable cause to search him since there was a bulge in his jacket which could have been a firearm.

The defendant disagreed and testified he was wearing the same jacket in court and took off his jacket and handed it to the judge to show him.

The judge examined the jacket and discovered a packet of cocaine in the jacket. The judge couldn't stop laughing at his discovery and called a short recess.

* "There shouldn't be a division of good people and bad people. People are actually either charming or tedious."

- Oscar Wilde

* A Detroit man watched on as police were showing school children their new car computer which located felons. The Detroit man stepped up and asked more about how it worked. The police asked him for his license and ran it through the computer and then arrested him for being wanted for an armed robbery in St. Louis two years earlier.

* If you think I'm funny or the things I say make you laugh, you should be aware I'm not trying to be funny. I am just a very bad and very mean person.

* There are bad people who are just like a dark cloud in the sky. When they leave the sky clears and it's a beautiful day.

* If you believe in Karma, you know whoever caused you harm will someday experience themselves the bad things they did to you.

Know also, there are people who believe in Karma yet feel Karma takes too long, so they will beat the sh*t out of you right away.

Barber Shop

* Joe walked into a barber shop and asked for a shave and a shoeshine.

The barber lathered his face and sharpened his large straight edge on a leather strap, while a beautiful young woman wearing a very low-cut top knelt in front of Joe and began to shine his shoes.

Joe's eyes bulged out as he just couldn't help glancing at her large quivering breasts as she brushed his shoes.

Joe started to laugh and said to the shoeshine girl, "You and I should get a room."

Unfazed, the beautiful young woman said, "My husband wouldn't like that."

Joe said, "What a waste! Tell your stupid husband you've got to work late, and I'll make it well worth your while."

Still unfazed, the beautiful woman continued to brush his shoes, and without looking up said, "You tell him. He's shaving you right now."

* The barber finished shaving Joe and showed him a bottle of after-shave lotion he was about to apply.

"No thanks, If I smell too pretty, my girlfriend probably will suspect I've been in a house of prostitution."

"Really?" Said the barber. "My wife doesn't seem to know anything about a house of prostitution smell."

Battle of the Sexes

* The battle of the sexes won't ever end if all the rubbing of elbows, socializing and consorting with the enemy continues.

- Henry Kissinger

* God watched Adam in the Garden of Eden and saw he was lonely, so God asked him, "What's wrong Adam?"

"God you made a great garden here, but I wish I had someone to talk to?"

God said, "Okay, I will create a woman who will be your companion and will make you happy. She will cook and take care of you, bear children and take care of the children all the time so you won't have a care in the world."

"Wow! That sounds pretty good so far, God."

God continued, "She will also be your best friend and she won't complain about anything, and she won't nag you. She will give her love freely to you, and she will cheer you all the time and will always greet you with a smile and serve you faithfully all the time."

"Well, that sound great, God! But what will a woman cost me?" Adam said.

"An arm and a leg," God said.

Adam thought about it a second and said, "What can I get for just a rib?"

* A homeless guy asked a lady for a dollar. The lady said, "A dollar! WTF? How about 75 cents? Because that's what a homeless lady would make doing the same job."

* Women who donate their eggs get paid thousands of dollars. Men can also donate their sperm, but they only get $50 or arrested all depending on where they donate.

* "Women are much superior to men," a woman said.

"What makes you say that?" A man replied.

"Everyone knows women live longer than men, have more tolerance than men, and are more considerate than men."

The man replied, "But God made Adam first. Men are first."

"Men are only the rough draft of what God had in mind before he made his final masterpiece."

* Sometimes I wonder how I put up with my wife. Then I remember she puts up with me.

* Joe looks up at his wife at the breakfast table and says, "A good cup of coffee is better than you in the morning."

"Why is that?" His wife asks.

"Coffee looks good in the morning and when coffee gets cold you can throw it away."

* Three men released a genie from a bottle and so the genie granted them each a wish.

The first man said, "OK, for my wish, I want my I.Q doubled." Immediately, the guy starts to recite complicated mathematical formulas and writes a symphony.

The second man asked the genie to triple his I.Q. Suddenly, he's speaking several languages some of which are ancient dialects. Then he solves complicated chemical engineering problems as well as complicated philosophical mysteries and theories of the universe.

Impressed, the last man asks the genie to increase his I.Q tenfold. The genie says, "Are you really sure that's what you want?"

"Yes, indeed!" He replies.

The genie replies, "Okay," and the man instantly turns into a woman.

* A man and a woman were competing against each other in a golf match for $20. When they finished at the 18th green, the lady lost but wanted to keep playing to win her $20 dollars back, so she pressed him to play three more golf holes for double or nothing.

It was getting dark and after finishing the additional 3 holes the lady lost and owed him $40. She wanted to play 3 more holes for double or nothing, but it was too dark. So, the man suggested they call it a day and have a drink to settle on his winnings.

She didn't want to lose and wanted one last bet. It was late, and no one was on the golf course. "Look," said the lady to the man. "We will have the last bet of the day double or nothing and add a $100 bonus to the winner."

The man asked, "What are we going to bet?"

"Let's see who can stream their pee the farthest." The man laughed and gladly agreed.

The lady took off her skirt and panties, squatted down and she began.

After she finished, the man measured it at two feet six inches.

The man began to unzip and got ready to begin when the woman stopped him.

"Hey! No free lift!"

* Women have more fun than men in this world which is because men have too many things which are forbidden to them.

- Oscar Wilde

* Men, if you want to have a woman love you, you should always tell her you love her, and you think about her. Buy her gifts now and then and give her flowers. Always listen to her when she speaks and always respect her.

Women, if you want a man to love you, have nothing on under your coat and carry a 12-pack of beer.

* The Lord watched Adam walking around in the Garden of Eden and called him out to tell him some news.

"Adam, I got two things to tell you. One is very good, and one is very bad." God said.

"Okay, God, please tell me your good news first," said Adam.

"I'm going to give you two new things which are a brain and a penis. You will be able to think for yourself, invent things and talk intelligently with Eve. The penis will give you much pleasure and Eve will also enjoy it very much."

"Great! So, what's the bad news?" Adam said.

"I'm sorry, Adam, but be aware you cannot use these two gifts simultaneously."

* A man is talking to God. "God, why did you make all women so gorgeous and beautiful?"

"So, you will like them."

"God, why did you make all women have such wonderful bodies shaped round and curvy?"

"So, you'll like them."

"So, God, why did you make all women so damn stupid?"

"Oh, that is so they will like you."

* A precocious young lad asked his father, "The teachers at school say I'm very smart – a brainy boy. Dad, you're a doctor so I must have got my smart brain from you?"

"Well, you must have got your brains from your mother, since I still have mine."

Big Butts

* I like big butts. I like a butt so big you can set up a small tv and a beer on it.

* 99 out of a hundred men like a woman with a big butt. The one-hundredth man prefers the other 99 men.

* Only trust a man who has gone on record that he likes a big butt since that is a man who cannot lie.

Or you can trust a man who says, "I express an immense amount of admiration and fondness for gargantuan derriere. I am neither deceiving you nor making any misrepresentations regarding this."

Be aware it may require a prodigious amount of imperturbability to converse with the latter and it's difficult to tell what the hell he's saying so it doesn't really matter if he's lying or not.

* I love my big butt and for those who think otherwise, they are welcome to kiss it.

* Joe went to a restaurant and ordered a bowl of chowder. The waitress brought it to the table but had her middle finger right in the chowder.

Joe scratched his head. "Miss you've got your finger in my chowder!"

"Oh, sorry. I've got rheumatism in my finger, and I try to keep it warm."

Joe got upset. "Well take your f*ckin' finger out of my chowder. Take it out now and bring me another bowl!"

The waitress went back to get a second bowl of chowder then returned to Joe's table and again, her finger is in the chowder.

"What the hell?" Joe said. "Take your f*ckin' finger out of the chowder and shove it up your fat ass!"

The waitress smiled and said, "I already tried that before I brought your second bowl of chowder out."

Brainy Humor

* A photon decides to visit his mother and travel by plane. As the photon goes through airport security, the officer asked him if he had any carryon bags or briefcase?

The photon told the officer he was traveling light.

* Helium gas walked into a restaurant. The maître 'd said, "I'm very sorry sir, but we don't allow any noble gasses in this restaurant."

Helium had no reaction.

* A bartender says, I don't serve anyone faster than the speed of light. Just then, a tachyon walked in and ordered a beer.

* Why did the dyslexic doubting Thomas toss and turn all night? He couldn't sleep since he wondered if there really a dog is.

* Can you find x?

Adult Joke Book for Men

AB=BC=CD=AD

x=?

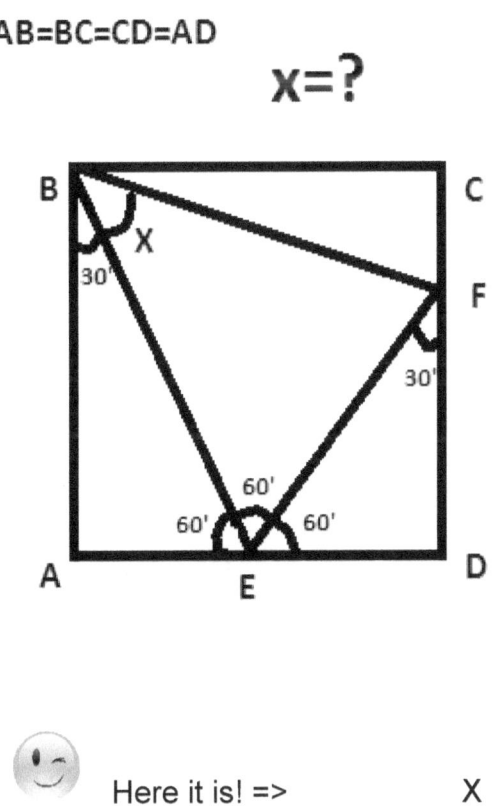

😉   Here it is! =>   X

* A mathematics professor, a medical doctor and an engineer had coffee in a street café. They watched people who entered and left a building.

They saw two people walk into the building, then a few minutes later, three people walked out of the building.

The doctor said, "They must have reproduced."

The engineer said, "A mistake was made in the count."

The math professor said, "If one more person goes into the house, it will be vacant."

* A neutron stopped into his neighborhood bar and sat down then ordered an ice-cold beer. The bartender saw him, gave him a beer and said, "Nice to see you again Neutron. What's new with you?"

"All good with me, but I'm thinking of moving to Switzerland."

"Hey that figures," said the bartender. "You don't seem like a guy who take sides and you'll fit it well there."

"Before I leave, I wanted to check on my tab. Do I owe you anything?"

"Hey, for you ol' buddy, there's no charge at all."

* It is difficult to talk to kleptomaniacs since they take things literally.

* I wanted to be clever but being funny came first. That's how you know someone is really clever if they can make a complicated joke very funny.

- Ricky Gervais

* An engineer, a math professor and a computer programmer are in a car and get a flat tire.

The engineer said, "We need to replace the car and buy a new car."

The math professor said, "We should take the flat tire off and buy a new tire."

The programmer said, "We should drive the car a mile or so and see if the tire fixes itself

* An Indian chief had three pregnant wives. The first wife had a boy, and the chief was so happy, he had a teepee built of the finest cowhide built for her.

The second wife also had a boy. The chief was so excited he also had another teepee built of finest cowhide for her.

The third wife gave birth shortly after that, but the chief didn't announce whether it was a boy or a girl. The chief had a huge teepee constructed which was much larger than the other two teepees and this teepee was made from the finest hide of a hippopotamus.

The chief posted a sign in their village announcing there would be a prize for whoever could guess the birth of the third wife.

No one could guess the result, but one young brave said the third wife had twin boys.

"How did you know that?" the chief asked him.

"It wasn't hard since… and in fact it was easy," said the brave. "The squaw of the hippopotamus is the same as the squaws of the other two hides."

Business

* Always borrow money from pessimists since they don't expect it back.

* If building a successful product is very difficult, time consuming, brain boggling and just plain hard to do, once you build the product, sell the process on how you built it, rather than the product.

* A small boy frequented a local barber shop. The barber was cutting Joe's hair when he noticed the boy about to visit his shop. The barber said to Joe, "This kid doesn't have both oars in the water. I'll show you what I mean."

The barber went to his register and pulled out two coins and a dollar bill. He put the dollar bill on one side of the table and two quarters on the other side. He said to the boy, "Help yourself son, but you can only take the money on one side of the table."

The boy smiled, took two quarters then walked out the door.

"See, he's not right."

A few days later, Joe ran into the kid coming out of a bank."

"Hey, kid! I've got to ask you. Why did you take two quarters when you could have had a dollar?"

The boy smiled and said, "Because the day I take the dollar the game's over."

* Knock Knock

Who's there?

Opportunity.

No way! Opportunity doesn't knock twice!

* If opportunity doesn't knock at your door, it's better to not wait around for a knock. Instead, work on building the door.

* The boss arrived driving a brand new bright red Ferrari. Joe went up to him in the parking lot and said, "Wow! That's an amazing car!"

Joe's boss put his hand on Joe's shoulder and said, "If you work hard, put in overtime when it's needed, and strive to be the best, I'll get another one for myself next year."

* Business opportunities are like buses, if you miss one, there's always another one coming.

- Richard Branson

* "The major problem with the entire world is too many people go on to grow up."

- Walt Disney

Cannibals and Comedians

* Two cannibals decided to catch, cook, and eat a clown. After cooking the clown, one cannibal said to the other, "Does this taste funny to you?"

* Years ago, Mr. Will Rogers said, "Everything is changing. People take comedians seriously and people take politicians as a joke.

Amazing how even more true that has become in present day.

* Comedians are sociologists since we point out stuff the public doesn't even stop to think about. We look at life in slow-motion and question everything we see.

- Steven Wright

* It is the duty if not the ultimate quest of a comedian to find out where the line is drawn, and then cross it deliberately.

- George Carlin

* According to Alexander Posey, an American poet, humorist, journalist, Comedians are people who embarrass themselves with class and style and bring a lot of joy to people.

Cars

* Ferdinand Porsche said, "I looked all around but I just couldn't find the right sports car. I dreamt about one which didn't need a lot of repairs all the time. So, I built one."

* Joe was speeding in his brand-new Porsche on a desert road when suddenly he was passed in a flash by a motorcyclist. He continued for a half-mile when he was pulled over by the police for speeding.

The officer handed Joe the citation, received his signature and was about to walk away when Joe asked, "Officer, I know I was speeding, but I don't think it's fair – did you see that motorcycle fly by me? Why did you give me the ticket and not him?"

"Ever go a-fishin'?" the policeman asked.

"Yeah, sure," Joe replied.

The officer grinned, "Did you ever catch 'em all?"

* Church officials discussed the nuisance of cell phones going off during church services. They decided to put a sign at the entrance which read:

"It is unlikely the Good Lord will call you on your mobile while you are here, so please turn it off before entering our Church. If you want to contact God, do so on your own in a quiet place where no one will disturb you. If you want to see God, just text him when you are driving a car."

* Joe walked into a car part store and said, "I need a gas cap for my Edsel."

The man behind the counter replied, "Sounds like a fair trade to me."

* When you see a man opening the car door for a woman, it can be two things: 1) a new car, or 2) a new wife.

- Prince Phillip

* A female penguin is driving through Arizona on summer vacation when something goes wrong with her car. She doesn't know what went wrong but manages to slowly drive the car into a small town and finds a gas station with a mechanic on duty.

She tells the mechanic what happened, and the mechanic says he'll look and see if he can find the problem.

The penguin meanwhile sees an ice cream parlor down the street and goes in and orders a dish of Vanilla Ice Cream Sunday, her favorite.

She doesn't have hands (just flippers) so she has difficulty eating it and spills it all over herself. She finishes, then returns to the gas station. The mechanic was hard at work under the car.

"Find anything," she asks?

The mechanic rolls out from under the car, and says, "Looks like you blew a seal."

"No, no." the penguin replies, "that's just a Vanilla Ice Cream Sunday."

* My wife is telling me she likes sex in the backseat of a car. Hey! Hey!

Then she tells me I'm the driver.

- Rodney Dangerfield

* A big-time Texas farmer sold his huge farm to a conglomerate, then he retired and took a trip to Europe and stopped in Romania which does about one-third of the farming in all of Europe, but the farms are small.

The farmer pulled over near a small Rumanian farm and waved to the farmer. After introducing himself as a tourist and a farmer, he asked the Rumanian to show him around his farm.

The Rumanian proudly showed the Texan his farm. "I grow crops here and keep my goats over here." The Rumanian continued showing the Texan everything about his small farm.

The Texan farmer couldn't believe how small the farm was and asked where the rest of his farm was.

"Oh, this is all I have for myself and my family," said the Rumanian.

"You sh*ttin' me? Said the Texan. "This is all?"

The farmer nodded yes.

"Well, boy, on my farm I could get in my car before dawn and I'd drive and drive, and by sunset, I'd only be halfway across my farm."

"Yes," said the Rumanian farmer, "I had a car like that too."

* Some people watch car races to see pile-ups and crashes. Statistics show you're safer in a race car than you are when you are traveling to and from the racetrack.

- Mario Andretti

* There's an unseen force, an invisible monster which lets birds know when you've just washed your car.

- Denis Norden

Chinese

* After a UN conference, delegations from England, France, China, and Japan took the same flight.

Suddenly, one of the engines quit, and the other engine was weakening. The captain announced the plane needed to lose weight.

Anything not bolted down inside the plane was tossed out.

Still, more weight needed to be lost. There were no parachutes on board.

The delegation from England shook everybody's hand and decided to sacrifice themselves and jumped out and yelled, "Long live the Queen!"

The plane still needed to lose weight and was descending uncontrollably.

The French delegation volunteered to jump next, and as they jumped they yelled, "Vive la France!"

Only the Chinese and Japanese delegation were left along with two pilots on the plane. The pilots announced, "We still need to lose weight the plane is losing serious altitude."

The Chinese ambassador yelled, "Long live the Peoples Republic of China!" …. And then kicked the Japanese delegation off the plane.

* A Chinese mother said to her son looking at his phone for hours, "Facebook? Why don't you face book and study?"

* A Chinese boy, whose parents made him study hard, told his dad, "Hey dad, I've got some bad news - I got Hepatitis B."

"Why only Hepatitis B? Why not Hepatitis A plus?"

* A Chinese guy walks into a bar and stands next to a guy and starts to drink.

The guy asks him, "Do you know martial arts like Kung Fu, Long Fist, Eagle Claw, Karate, ah, you know what I mean?"

The Chinese man turns to him and says, "Why the hell do you ask me that? Is it because I'm CHINESE!"

"No, it's because you're drinkin' my f*ckin' beer."

* A Chinese teenager asked his father how much it would cost to get married. His father said, "I don't know son, I'm still paying."

- Well-known Chinese joke.

* If there was only pasta and Chinese food in this world, I'm okay.

- Michael Chang, Tennis star and International Tennis Hall of Famer

* Joe and his wife go into a Chinese restaurant and his wife likes the design of Chinese characters on the menu. She takes the menu home and designs a shirt with the large well-designed characters displayed on it.

She wears it frequently until one day, a Chinese lady stopped her and asked her if she knew what her shirt said. Joe's wife replied, "No."

"Your shirt says, 'Cheap but good.'"

* Stephen King mentioned one of the most amazing things he's ever seen in his life is the Great Wall of China which was built one stone at a time. He remarked, it is so huge astronauts Eugene Cernan and Ed Lu have seen the wall from space without a telescope. This wall is a creation built just one stone at a time.

Kind of the like what Confucius said, "The longest journey begins with a single step."

Consultants

* Scott Adams, the creator of Dilbert Comic Strips, said consultants have credibility because they aren't dumb enough to work at your company.

* Joe preferred to con people and insult people, so he became a consultant.

* A surgeon, a civil engineer, and a consultant discussed what each thought was the earliest skill.

The doctor said, "Well, God had to remove a rib from Adam and put the rib in Eve and that is surgery. So, surgery is the oldest skill."

The engineer disagreed. "Before that, the book of Genesis describes God created the heavens and earth out of chaos. That took massive engineering skills, so civil engineering is the oldest profession in the world."

The consultant smiled, then got up and walked around the room and confidently said, "Aha! You both agree the earth was created out of chaos. Who do you think created the chaos?"

* A dog breeder was having trouble keeping dogs from fighting with each other and had to separate them otherwise they would sometimes fight to the death. So, the breeder hired a consultant to solve the problem.

"Add potassium nitrate to their diet and that will calm them down," said the consultant.

After a week, the breeder went back to the consultant and complained, "The dogs are still fighting, and I've lost a few of them now. What do I do?

"Add cranberry juice to their drinking water and that will surely help," said the consultant.

Another week went by, and the breeder went back to the consultant. "My dogs are still fighting and I'm still losing them. I don't know what the hell to do?"

"Oh, I have more suggestions for you," the consultant advised. "But before we discuss this further, do you have any more dogs? We need to determine that first."

* Give someone a fish, and you will be feeding the person for a day.

If you teach a man to fish, you'll lose him as a prospect if you were trying to sell him fish, or he'll buy a lot of fishing gear, chest waders, ridiculous hats, and a truck to haul it all.

But if you talk to a person who is starving about fish, then you are a consultant.

- Scott Adams

* A glass with 50% water in it was on a table. The optimist said, "It's half full."

The pessimist said, "It's half empty."

The consultant said, "It's two times as big as need be."

Courtship

"Laughing connects you socially. You can't be reserved or be distant when you are roaring with laughter."

- John Cleese

* Women fake orgasms to have relationships. Men fake relationships to have orgasms.

* Joe was a single guy who played golf every Saturday with his usual group. Joe admired an extremely attractive and sexy woman who usually practiced by herself on the driving range at the same time Joe's group teed off. Every other guy at the golf club admired this woman too.

Joe lusted for her. Infatuated with this woman, Joe wanted to meet her desperately. He wanted to talk to her, but she was way out of his league, and he couldn't get the courage to go up and talk with her.

He looked around the golf club searching for her every time he was there. He asked about her, but no one knew who she was. Joe spent sleepless nights thinking about how he could approach this gorgeous woman.

One-night Joe had a dream. In the dream, he was hitting balls on the practice range but this time he pulled out of his golf bag a magic bright fluorescent orange driver, brighter in color than any driver he'd ever seen. It looked magnificent. In his dream, Joe instantly appeared on the driving range hitting golf balls with this amazing orange driver farther than he'd ever hit golf balls in his life.

While he was hitting huge shots with his magic driver, the beautiful woman approached him.

"Excuse me." She said. "I couldn't help but notice the orange driver you are using."

"Oh, hello! You are very welcome to try it yourself. Here try it and you'll be amazed by the difference in distance," Joe said. Joe politely handed her the driver and she smiled and tried it. Sure enough, the gorgeous woman hit balls even further than Joe.

After several shots, they began to talk, and Joe politely introduced himself. "My name is Joe. I've seen you here practicing every Saturday and wanted to meet you. But no one here at the club seems to know who you are?"

"Oh, yes. My name is Vanessa." Her sweet sexy voice made Joe yearn with desire. Vanessa continued talking to Joe in his dream, and Joe focused on her beautiful red lips as she mouthed her words to him in a dreamy slow motion.

Vanessa paused hitting more balls and said to Joe, "I'm cursed with being so attractive. Men keep bothering me -- interrupting me. I try to keep to myself, it's better that way. The attention I get is sooo annoying."

"Aaah, you have my sympathy, and I understand exactly how you feel. A true gentleman like myself understands how annoying that can be to a beautiful woman like yourself."

Joe continued, "You certainly are a great golfer and incredibly attractive. My sister has the same problem – fighting away men all the time. Here, why don't you practice with this driver more and I'll hit over there. If you want to borrow it for a week or more, that would be fine with me. Just give it back to me when you're finished. For now, I'll stand here so no one will bother you."

"Why thank you! You are a gentleman and a genuinely nice person."

Joe smiled and after the beautiful woman finished hitting Joe's magic driver they began to talk more, and they got along so well, Joe found the courage to ask her out for dinner and she happily accepted.

They went to dinner and had a wonderful time getting to know each other. This was one of the best dreams Joe ever had.

"Briiiinggg!" Joe's alarm went off and he jumped out of bed. Today was Saturday and he didn't waste any time getting his driver and carefully painted the head on his driver a bright fluorescent orange and rushed out with the orange driver early to the range and began to hit balls just as he did in his dream.

Then Joe noticed out of the corner of his eye the gorgeous woman was walking up to hit balls on the range. Just like in his dream, the gorgeous woman noticed Joe's orange driver and went up to talk to him.

"Excuse me." She said. "I couldn't help but notice the bright orange driver you are using."

"Yes… Hecka hech," Joe began with a throaty, nervous laugh, "Do you want to f*ck?"

* Women are attracted to men with money and many men say if they had a dollar for every woman that found them unattractive, they would eventually find them attractive.

* If he's not calling you, it's because he's not thinking of you. Women need to realize in general men aren't bothered by disappointing you. If he says he's busy he's not respecting you. "Busy" is another word for "sh*thead." "Sh*thead" is another word for the guy you're dating. You deserve a f*cking phone call."

- Greg Behrendt

* A young mans dated a new girl for two months and drove her back to her house after their first date. When they reached the front door, the young guy stuck his chest out and leaned with one hand against the wall and said, "Sweetie, why don't you give me a BJ?"

"What? Are you crazy!" she said?

"Look, don't worry," he said. "It will be quick, I promise you."

"Nooo! Someone may see us, a neighbor, anybody..."

"Honey, at this time of the night no one will show up. C'mon, sweetie, I really need it."

"I've already said NO, and NO is final!"

"Baby, it'll just be very quick."

"NO!!! I've said NO!!!"

Desperately, the young guy said, "My love, don't be like that. I promise you I love you and I really need this BJ."

At that moment, the older sister showed up at the door in her nightgown half asleep.

Rubbing her eyes, she said, "Dad said, 'Dammit, give him the BJ or I'll have to blow him. But for God's sake, tell your boyfriend to take his hand off the intercom button so the rest of the family can get some sleep.'"

* I prefer ordinary girls - you know, college students, waitresses, that sort of thing. Most of the girls I go out with are just good friends. Just because I go out to the cinema with a girl, it doesn't mean we are dating.

- Leonardo DiCaprio

* A young man strode into a pharmacy and asked for a packet of condoms. The pharmacist replied, "They come in packs. How many do you want?"

"Well," the young man began confidently, "I've been seeing this girl and she's really hot. I want the condoms because I think I'm going to need them tonight. We're having dinner with her parents, and then we're going away for the weekend. Once she has seen what I'm like in the sack, she'll want me all the time. So, you'd better give me a dozen. Yeah, that's right, some of those ribbed ones that glow in the dark and a few of those with the Devil's heads on the end."

The pharmacist handed over the condoms, and the young man left, grinning ear to ear.

Later that evening, he sat down to dinner with his girlfriend and her parents. Before they began, he asked if they could say grace. The family agreed but were taken aback when the young man continued praying silently for several minutes after grace had finished.

His girlfriend leaned over and whispered, "You never told me you were so religious."

The young man leaned back and whispered, "You never told me that your father was a pharmacist!"

* Whenever I first start dating a guy, I say to myself, "Is this the man I want my children to spend their weekends with?"

- Rita Rudner

*Charlie got tired of chasing women and decided he was going to date one lady at a time and never fool around again. He met a wonderful woman and had been dating her exclusively for the past three years.

They did everything together. Charlie and his steady lady were shopping in the supermarket when Charlie noticed a very beautiful young woman smiling and waving at him. A bit perplexed, Charlie took his lady by the hand and walked over to the young woman.

"Hello!" The young woman said.

Charlie scratched his head, "Do you know me?"

"Yes, you are the father of one of my children."

Charlie, wide-eyed, started to walk away. Then he stopped, smacked his forehead, and blurted out, "My Lord! Are you the dancer at the Vegas bar I was in about 6 months ago who took me in the backroom, and I made love to you in the dark while your naked girlfriends massaged me?"

The young woman said, "No, I'm your son's teacher."

* Joe was single and doing his own grocery shopping and found a note left in an empty grocery cart which was written in beautiful very feminine handwriting which said, "Popcorn, beer and sh*t like that." Joe took the note and searched the parking lot hoping to find his true soul mate.

* Joe finished his round and went to the clubhouse for a beer. He sat down and saw a huge ugly fat guy talking to a very attractive woman.

Suddenly the girl slapped the huge man. The huge guy turned back to his beer laughing. To his amazement, the girl and the huge guy are now suddenly getting along very well again and left the bar together.

A few days go by, and Joe walked into the clubhouse bar after another round and the same scenario repeats itself - with the huge fat guy, this time talking with a different gorgeous girl. He sees the same thing unfold and the beautiful girl slaps him. The fat guy then says something, and the girl melts and they leave the bar together.

A week later Joe walks into the clubhouse but the huge ugly guy is sitting by himself. Joe walked up to the guy and said, "I see you in here hooking up with beautiful women and, well . . . you must have a very unusual method for doing it . . . what's your secret?"

The guy says, "I really shouldn't tell you, it's a family secret."

"Please, I've got to know."

"Okay, since I'm leaving town tomorrow I'll tell you. What I do is tell her something extremely offensive like, 'tickle your crotch with a feather?' and the girl usually freaks out or slaps me.

And then I say "Whoa, whoa! All I said was, "I'm a grouch with bad weather." At which point she feels guilty for having slapped me. I use that guilt to get her into bed with me."

Joe replied, "and that works for you?"

"Yeah, every time, the guy replies. "Go try it yourself!"

So, Joe gets off the barstool and walked up to the hottest girl in the bar, tapped her on the shoulder and she turned around.

"Slap your p*ssy with a nine iron?" Joe said.

The woman looks astonished and says, WHAT DID YOU SAY?!"

Joe replied, "All I said was, it is f*cking raining outside."

* Joe met a single girl at a party and asked her why she was still single.

"Why am I single? Well, I really don't know why? I'm a great chef. I love to laugh and have fun. I enjoy sex and I'm a caring faithful person. And, if that doesn't interest you, look at my gorgeous butt. If my butt doesn't sell you, maybe you should look for someone on the other team?

Or, perhaps you would get a more accurate answer to your question if you asked all the people who wouldn't date me?"

* A handsome and very well-dressed man shopped at the grocery store and ran his cart into an attractive woman as he turned the aisle.

"Oh, excuse me, I've very sorry." He said. "I've got my mind on other things and not paying attention."

"What's on your mind?" She asked.

"Oh, I'm cruising the world in a yacht I've chartered and I'm getting a few more things before I cruise out." The man said.

"You know, this is very strange, but you look like exactly my third husband."

"Is that so? How many times have you been married?"

"Twice," she replied.

* I was talking to a young woman in the clubhouse bar last night. She said, "If you lost a few pounds, had a shave, and got your hair cut, you'd look all right."

I said, "If I did that, I'd be talking to your friends over there instead of you."

* Joe had no social life, so his sister set him up for a blind date with a friend of hers from a nearby college.

His sister told him, "She's quiet, beautiful, and a happy person who doesn't get out much either, like you, brother dear. I think you will like her!"

Joe reluctantly agreed. "Where should I take her?" He asked his sister.

"Take her to the Carnival. There are lots of things to do with lots of people there and you two loners will have lots of fun."

So, Joe picked her up and took her to the carnival. The girl was even more beautiful than his sister described. Joe tried as hard as he could to get her to talk, but she kept to herself and didn't say much and remained quiet and shy.

Joe asked asks her as they approached the carnival ticket office, "What do you want to do first?"

She stared at him a while and said, "I want to get weighed."

He took her over to "Guess Your Weight Within 5 lbs."

"125 lbs.?" The carnie guessed.

Then she got on the scale and weighed 115 lbs. and won a teddy bear.

Joe then took her on the Tilt-A-Whirl Ride and when they got off, he asked her what she wanted to do.

"How about I get weighed." She said.

So, Joe took her to the same "Guess your Weight" but since the carnie knew what she weighed, they didn't win a prize and Joe wasted $5.

They continued to walk around, and Joe asked her what she wanted to do next.

"I just want to get weighed." She said.

Joe was exasperated. He figured there had to be something wrong with this girl. Joe doesn't say anything and drove her back to her college dorm. Joe gave her a brief handshake and said, "Goodnight."

The blind date walked to her room and her roommate, Lorretta, asked her how her blind date went.

The blind date said, "Oh, Worretta, it was reary wousy."

* Excellent single men and women are very hard to find. If the truth be told, they are usually still at work diligently working after hours. Search offices still lit after 7pm for the good ones. – Anon.

* The beauty of online dating is you can pick and choose without having to go outside or spend money.

* The late Oscar winning actor, Heath Ledger, said, "I enjoy dating older women because they don't pretend or try to act older like younger women do. Older women try to act younger, and I enjoy that."

Criticism

* Bob Saget, one of the stars of the hit series "Full House" pointed out the demographics of people who watched the show, "Full House," were 10-year-old kids.

When the show first came out, the critics hated the show. They said it was terrible and Bob Saget was worthless. Bob Saget didn't understand why the big newspapers didn't ask 10-year-old kids for their opinion instead of "having a 50-year-old guy from a big newspaper say Saget was a piece of crap."

* Chelsea Handler discussed a politer way for a critic to express a critical opinion. In a review of the movie, "Good Luck Chuck" which was a comedy starring Dane Cook and Jessica Alba, one tactful critic said the movie had all the belly laughs you have come to expect from Jessica Alba, but said absolutely nothing about Dane Cook.

* Some say when Arnold Schwarzenegger entered politics, he wouldn't be elected since he just had a name for himself with no political experience.

But George W. Bush was the same and so was Donald Trump.

Perhaps the days of career politicians ("those that can't make it in the real world enter politics") may be coming to an end. Independent critics serve us to make us aware of who we are voting for.

The greatest thing overall is that we can freely express opinions. Whether anyone listens to us is another matter, and the more independent and trustworthy you are, the more people seem to listen to you.

* An Aussie golfer was talking to his barber while getting a new haircut for his upcoming trip to The Masters in 2013 and was very excited about the trip to watch the Tournament.

The barber asked, "Mate? Why would you want to go to the US? Customs is all buggered up, you'll be standing in ques for hours and hours, still tired from a long flight?"

"We're going through LAX on Qantas."

"LAX is the worst, and Qantas? Mate? They're bad news in my opinion. The flights are always late, you're going to get cold food and the flight attendants are ugly and slow."

The barber continued cutting, "It's better to watch the Master's on TV, mate. It's too crowded at the Tournament. You'll be standing 4 rows back and won't see much. You've got to stand in long lines for all the portaloos. Save your money. On TV, you can see all the action, you can see the players up close, interviews - the latest on everything. Where are you staying?"

"The tour guide has that all arranged."

"Yeah right! Tour guide, Haha! Sure. He'll give you each a pillow and put you both in a toilet and charge you for the Taj Mahal, mate. The tour guide is using you for an ATM machine."

Six weeks later, the guy returned after the trip for another haircut. The barber asked him how it went.

"It was wonderful, the golf was fantastic! Not only were we on time in one of Qantas' brand-new planes, but it was overbooked, and they bumped us up to first class. The food and wine were wonderful, and I had a beautiful flight attendant wait on my wife and me hand and foot. She even brought us a night-cap."

"We got through LAX easily – no problem."

"And the hotel was great! They'd just finished a $30 million renovation, and it's the finest place in the area. The hotel was overbooked, so they gave us the Presidential Suite at no extra charge! We even had a butler who accompanied us to the golf tournament and waited on us, all compliments of the hotel!"

"Well," muttered the barber, "You just got very lucky. But I know you didn't see any of the player interviews?"

"We followed Adam Scott and his caddy, Steve Williams. The butler made sure we were always up front, and we could see everything! We even saw the bloke's putt go in on the second playoff hole to win it!" He continued. "When Adam and Steve walked off the green after the celebration, the bloke noticed us and told something to Steve, and Steve came over and talked with us."

"What the hell?" Said the barber.

"Yeah, it's true! Steve told us Adam was so grateful for our support - he knew we were Aussies when he heard us cheer. He wanted to show his appreciation to us, and Steve said Adam invited us to go with him into the clubhouse to see him receive his first green jacket."

"Really?" Said the barber.

"So, we went into the clubhouse with Adam and witnessed him getting his green jacket. Then Adam came up to my wife and I and talked with me."

"Wow! Really? What did he say to you?"

He said, "Who f*cked up your hair?"

* Do what you feel in your heart and mind to be the right thing to do since whether it is good or bad, you'll be criticized anyway.

- Eleanor Roosevelt

* When the well-known opera, "Carmen" premiered in 1875, the critics lambasted it – by severely and savagely criticizing it. It only lasted 45 performances. Critics called it a "musical and moral outrage."

After Carmen composer, Georges Bizet, died at age 37, "Carmen" began its climb to worldwide fame.

If you believe in your creation, and the rest of the world is laughing or yelling "Boo," just don't give up.

- Karen DeCrow, a late lawyer, author, and activist, best known for work in equal rights for men in child custody cases.

Dark Humor

* Caution grim humor: An Alaskan wife whose husband loved fishing didn't come home at his normal time after his early morning fishing.

The wife became worried after she woke up the next morning to a knocking at this front door. She opened the door to see two policemen standing there.

"We're very sorry Ma'am, but we have information about your husband," said one of the men.

"What is it! Where's my husband?"

One policeman said, "Sorry, but we have some bad news, and we have some good news. And, besides that, we do have some fantastic news."

"Tell me the bad news first," the wife said.

"We are very sorry to tell you this, but we found your husband's body. Seems he accidentally drove into the sea and drowned."

"Oh my God!" exclaimed the wife. Swallowing hard, she asked, "If that is the bad news, what the heck is the good news?"

The trooper continued, "When we pulled him up, he had 10 of the largest Alaskan King Crabs we've ever seen on him. Haven't seen King Crabs that big for many years, and we believe you should share in the catch."

"Oh my God, that's the good news? What the hell is the fantastic news?"

The trooper replied, "We're gonna pull him up again to check for more crabs tomorrow."

* Caution grim humor: A very avid fisherman was having the best fishing day of his life when his mobile phone began to vibrate.

It was his doctor's office. The doctor's office was calling him to tell him that his wife had just been in a terrible accident and was in critical condition, and in ICU at the hospital.

The man told the doctor's office to tell the doctor to inform his wife he was out in a boat fishing, but he'd be right there!

As he finished his call, he hooked a massive fish that took out most of his line. The hospital wasn't that far away, and he thought there wasn't much he could do at the hospital anyway. So, he decided to just get this big one in then beeline to the hospital.

He fought the fish for two hours and finally got it into the boat. Then he motored ashore and ran to his car and drove to the hospital still wearing his fishing gear and feeling very guilty.

He parked at the hospital and jogged up to the entrance. As soon as he came through the doors, he saw his doctor standing there. "How is my wife doing," the golfer asked.

His doctor, who was a long-time fishing buddy glared at him and shouted, "Where were you?! Did you continue fishing?"

The man couldn't lie and hung his head nodding that he kept fishing.

"Well, while you were out enjoying your fishing, your wife has been going through a lot in the ICU!"

The doctor continued, "I hope you had a great time because that's the last time you'll be going fishing for a while."

The doctor shook his head. "Your wife will require round the clock care from now on, so you won't be doing much else while you'll be caregiving for her."

The fisherman was feeling so guilty he broke down sobbing and crying uncontrollably.

The doctor then laughed and said, "I'm just kidding. She's dead. What'd you catch?"

* A masochist and a sadist teamed up for a Two-Man Better Ball Golf tournament. They almost won the whole tournament, but the masochist sadly missed a very easy one-foot putt to win everything on the 18th green then missed the putt coming back as well.

The masochist pleaded and pleaded with his sadist partner, "Please hurt me… hurt me for missing that short putt!"

The sadist considered it, then said, "No."

* A broke tourist hired a hooker in Panama. He paid her and for laughs he said to her as he drove away, "Moneyo counterfito!"

She yelled back, "Syphilis autentico!"

* Years ago, Joe was on holiday in Africa. Going through the African bush, he encountered a young bull elephant with its front leg raised and it was bleeding on the ground.

Approaching carefully, Joe saw a piece of wood stuck in the elephant's foot. Joe patted the elephant's leg and gently pulled the wood out with pliers. The elephant carefully placed its injured foot back on the ground.

The elephant turned to Joe and stared at him for some time. Then the large elephant quietly walked away.

Years later, Joe visited a park zoo. As he approached the elephants, one large elephant turned and came out toward Joe.

When the elephant got to the fence, it stared at Joe for a long time even though others were standing next to him. The elephant lifted one of its front feet off the ground in a sequential pattern.

Remembering the encounter years ago, Joe wondered if this was the same elephant. He thought about it, then bravely climbed over the railing, and made his way toward the elephant.

The elephant trumpeted once more, then slowly wrapped its trunk around one of Joe's legs and slammed him against the railing breaking most of the bones in his body.

Joe remarked in the ambulance, it probably wasn't the same f*ckin' elephant.

* Joe told his lawyer, "My ex-wife's been following me around all morning."

His lawyer replied, "She's still wants something from you, Joe. You had a lot of trouble with her, and if you show any interest in her, she's going to cling to you like a colony of E. Coli, and you are room-temperature Kobe beef until she gets what she's after."

* Caution: grim humor. If I were a serial killer, I would like to have the name, 'The Suspense' so when they said, 'The suspense is killing me,' we would both have a great laugh. Then I would kill them.

* Caution: This one is very bad and go on to the next joke if you have a weak stomach.

Wolfman and Dracula walk into a bar. They sit down, and the bartender says, "Hi guys! Glad to have you back. What'll you have?"

Wolfman says, "I want a beer and the biggest bloodiest steak you got!"

"Comin' right up. How about you Drac?"

"I'll just have cup of hot water."

Bartender looks puzzled. Wolfman says, "What the hell? You just having hot water?"

Dracula pulls out a used tampon, "It's teatime."

Desert Island

* If you ever asked me what book I would like to have with me if I ever became stranded on a desert island, I would bring a book on how to build a boat.

- Steven Wright

* Three guys on a deserted island in the middle of the ocean find a magic lantern. They rub it and a genie pops out and granted each of them one wish.

The first guy said, "Get me off this island and get me home." In an instant, he was gone."

The second guy wished the same and likewise disappeared.

The third guy said, "Hey! It's lonely here. I wish to have my friends back here."

(Sorry, we know that's a corny joke but thought it might be useful for a silly comment on last man standing conversations.)

* Somebody once told me I treated my smartphone like Wilson, the volleyball Tom Hanks turns into a friend when he's stranded on a desert island in that movie "Castaway."

It's a fair comparison since if you are raising little ones you feel like you have been stranded on a dessert island and the only connection with the real world is your phone.

- Rachel Simmons

* Joe was stranded on a desert island with the famous actress, Jennifer Lawrence, and was very polite and treated her as best as he could. As time passed, he asked if she would like to have sex with him to help their physical requirements.

Not knowing if they would ever get off the island, Jennifer agreed, and they enjoyed a great physical relationship.

As time passed more, Joe said, "Jennifer, this is a kind of a guy thing, but can you do a favor for me?"

She said, "Ok".

Joe said, "May I borrow your eyebrow pencil?"

Jennifer, confused by the request, nevertheless gave him the pencil.

Joe continued, "May I draw a mustache on you?" Jennifer was still confused but agreed and Joe drew a mustache on her.

"May I ask you to wear some of my clothes, so you would look manlier?" Joe said.

Jennifer was getting a bit upset but tried on some of Joe's clothes.

After she put on the clothes, Joe said, "Do you mind if I call you 'Jack?'"

Jennifer had to see where this was going. "Yes, you can call me Jack."

Joe put his arm on Jennifer's shoulder and said, "Jack, you won't believe who I'm f*cking."

Doctors

* Joe took a trip to Russia and loved the Russian women. But after he got back to the US he

noticed his dick was swollen and was covered in orange spots, so he went to the doctor.

The doctor did some tests and when the tests came back he told Joe he had a rare Siberian Venereal Disease they didn't know very much about and didn't have a cure and couldn't treat it. The doctor suggested amputation.

"What! Not me! That's crazy! How about penicillin?"

"Penicillin won't do anything, Joe. We need to remove it." The doctor said.

Joe didn't like that, so he went to see a Russian Doctor.

The Russian doctor looked at Joe's penis and said, "Comrade, you have rare form of SVD - Siberian Venereal Disease with the orange spots."

"Yes, that is what my other doctor told me. He was going to amputate, and I want to avoid that."

The Russian doctor laughed. "They always want to amputate! Comrade, it's strictly capitalistic greed. They know they make more money if they amputate. You don't need amputation."

"Great! That's wonderful!" Joe said.

"Yes, do not worry comrade. Just wait for one more week. Don't listen to the greedy American doctors if they say you need amputation. Your dick will fall off by itself and you'll save money."

* If you walk into a doctor's office and notice all the plants have died, you should turn around and find another doctor.

- Erma Bombeck

* Joe went to a psychiatrist and told the doctor he was depressed. Joe believed his life was boring, difficult, and cruel. He felt like things were caving in on him due to the overwhelming uncertainty in life itself.

The doctor said, "I know what you need. There is a clown convention in town, and they are putting on hilarious shows. If you go there tonight, there is show featuring 'Bananas the Clown' and he's hilarious! Go and see his show, relax, enjoy yourself, and forget about things for a while. Oh, and I don't want to prescribe drugs, they're only artificial and temporary. Go see the show and that will get you out of your depressed mood."

Joe, surprisingly, was sobbing away. "What's wrong," the psychiatrist asked?

"But Doc, I am 'Bananas the Clown."

* An orthopedic surgeon was sitting in his office when a young woman walked in unexpectedly. "What do you want," the surgeon asked her?

"Doctor, I think I am a dog."

"Miss, I'm an orthopedic surgeon and I think you need to see a psychiatrist."

The woman replies, "Yes, doctor, I already am aware that I should see a psychiatrist."

"Well why then did you walk into my office?"

"Someone threw a ball this way."

* An engineer was removing the engine parts from a motorcycle when he saw a famous heart surgeon in his repair shop.

He said to the doctor, "Look at this great engine... I opened its heart, took the valves out, repaired it all and put all the parts back. So, why do I get such a small salary and you get huge sums?"

The doctor smiled at the engineer and said. "Let's see if you can do the same while the engine is running."

"Oh? okay," said the engineer. "But if the engine's not running and I've got the parts spread out all over, I can get that engine running again. Can you?"

   * A beautiful blonde woman walked into the doctor's office and the doctor became infatuated with her stunning looks. The doctor couldn't help himself and told her to take off her pants.

She did, and the doctor started rubbing her thighs.

"Do you know why I'm doing this procedure," asked the doctor?

"Yes, checking for abnormalities." She replied.

He told her to take off her blouse and bra which she did.

The doctor began rubbing her breasts and asked, "Do you know what this procedure is?"

"Yes, checking for cancer."

The doctor told her to take off her panties, then he laid her on the table, and began making love to her.

"Do you know what is going on now?" The doctor moaned with pleasure.

"Yes, getting herpes -- that's why I am here!"

* A man walked into a sperm bank and declared, "I'm one of the wealthiest men in the world and have an I.Q. of 165, and I'd like to make a donation."

The nurse gave him a sealed cup and directed him to a private room. A long time passed, and the man was still in the private room.

The nurse knocked on the door and said, "Is there a problem?"

"I'm sorry, I'm so embarrassed, I used my right hand. I used my left hand. I poured cold water on it and hot water on it. I banged it against the counter, I shook it…. Could you help me?"

The nurse replied, "I don't usually do this, but it would be my pleasure."

She knelt and began to give him a BJ.

"Nurse, now I'm not saying I don't really appreciate this, but I just need help getting the cap off the jar."

* A blonde complained to her doctor in his office, "Doctor, my husband and I have been trying to have a baby, but we just can't. What's wrong?"

"Okay, take your clothes off and lie down," said the doctor.

"Alright, but I was hoping to have the baby with my husband."

* Grim humor: A professor in a forensic pathology class was giving an introductory lecture to his students. Standing over a corpse, he addressed the class. "There are two things you need to make a career in medical forensics.

First, you must be daring and have courage."

After he said that, he shoved a finger up the corpse's rear end and raised it up then licked it, and said, "Now you must do the same," he told the class.

After a pregnant pause, the students did what the professor just told them.

"Second," the professor continued, "you must have an acute sense of observation. Did any of you notice I put my little finger in this man's anus, but put my index finger in my mouth?"

* A Patient consulted his doctor and told him he was sick and depressed. The doctor said, "You should cut down on drinks."

"But I don't touch a drop," the patient said.

"Then you should cut down on smoking."

"But I don't smoke."

"Then you should stop taking drugs."

The patient answered, "I don't do drugs."

"Then you should cut down on womanizing."

"I haven't chased women in my life."

The doctor paused then said, "In that case, go to bar and have a shot and beer, smoke a fine cigar and try some marijuana too. Then take a few girls home with you."

* A wife was complaining about shortness of breath and her husband took her to the doctor. After meeting with the doctor, the wife told the husband her problem was she had attractive genitalia.

"What?" Her husband was outraged.

He barged in on the doctor and said, "What's this about you telling my wife she had attractive genitalia?"

"I didn't say that." Said the doctor. "I said she has acute angina."

* It always pays to be extra nice to receptionists, nurses, and all the doctor's staff for prevention against the doctor accidentally killing you.

* A toast to a doctor: Here's to my doctor who explained to me I wasn't really dying and f*ck the website which convinced me I was."

* A heart surgeon passed away with a very fancy funeral. A family donated a ten-foot heart made up of roses which was placed behind the casket.

When the service finished, the casket was solemnly and slowly wheeled through the heart made of roses and into his final resting place. The heart then automatically closed in on the casket sealing the casket forever.

One of the mourners couldn't help but break out in laughter. Then he quickly recovered and said, "I'm very sorry. That beautiful heart sealing made me think of my own funeral ceremony. You see, I'm a gynecologist."

Another mourner, a proctologist, left suddenly.

Employment

* Time varies when you have a job.

You wake up every morning at 6 am and you close your eyes for just ten minutes and the next thing you know it's 7 am.

But, when you're at work and you get off at 5 pm and its 4 pm and you close your eyes for what you think is ten minutes, but when you open your eyes it's 4:01 pm.

* A man was headhunted by a large firm and agreed to take on a major role in a very large multinational company. On his first day, he dialed the cafeteria and shouted into the phone: "Get me a f*ckin' cup of coffee and get it here quick!"

The voice from the other side replied, "You fool, you've dialed the wrong extension! Do you have any idea in the world who you are talking to?"

"No," replied the new man.

"This is the CEO, idiot!"

The new man shouted back, "And do you know who YOU are f*ckin' talking to, you f*ckin' dickhead?"

"No," replied the CEO.

"Good!" replied the new man and immediately terminated the call.

* Emily Swanson remained a housekeeper for over 40 years for the family of John Kenneth Galbraith a well-known US economist.

One afternoon in the 1960s, her character and devotion toward Kenneth Galbraith was tested.

It has been a tiring day for Ken Galbraith, after which he and his wife were supposed to attend a dinner party. Ken asked his housekeeper Emily to hold all telephone messages while he took a quick power nap.

Shortly thereafter, the phone rang, and it was President Lyndon Johnson, who said to Emily, "Get me Ken Galbraith. This is Lyndon Johnson."

"He is sleeping, Mr. President. He has said not to disturb him," Emily replied.

Johnson kept insisting to talk with him and told her she definitely needed to get him on the phone.

Emily said, "No, Mr. President, I work for him, not you."

A few hours later Galbraith learned about Johnson's call and quickly called the President back – a bit nervous.

Johnson laughed and said, "Tell that woman I want her here, working for me in the White House."

    * Chose a lazy person to do a difficult job because he will find an easy way to do it.

    - Bill Gates

    * A young woman thought to herself, *I'm sick of this job. I'm going to quit and make big money as a stripper.* Then she remembered she can't dance.

    * Tell me, what is your dream job?

A. In my dreams, I don't work.

* During a job interview, the applicant was told by the sales manager, "I want you to try and sell this laptop to me," and handed the laptop to the applicant.

The applicant picked up the laptop, turned and walked out of the interview. The sales manager thought the applicant was preparing a great sales pitch but when the applicant didn't return, the manager called him.

"Where'd you go? I need the laptop," said the manager.

"I'll sell it back to you for $50."

Engineers

* Engineers solve problems you didn't know you had in ways you don't understand anyway.

* Two engineering students were talking on campus. One had a brand-new bike. The other student asked him where he got it.

"I was here on campus when a beautiful co-ed rode up to me with this bike. Then she put the bike down and stripped naked and said, "Have it your way and take whatever you want."

The first engineering student said, "Great decision. Her clothes wouldn't have fit you."

* Try giving college grads out in the wilderness where they are away from modern convenience a massive amount of marijuana and nothing to smoke it in.

You will be amazed at how fast they become engineers.

* A wife asked her engineer husband, "Could you please go shopping for me and buy one coffee cake, and if they have eggs, get 6!"

A short time later the husband comes back carrying six coffee cakes.

The wife asked him, "Why on earth did you buy six coffee cakes for the two of us?"

"They had eggs."

   * An unemployed engineer graduate was looking out for a suitable job. He went to many personal interviews, only to be rejected.

Being fed up with so many months of his job hunt, he decided to take any job he could get.

He visited a circus group and asked for a job. But the owner said that there wasn't any job for his education level, but there was a vacancy to act as a monkey and entertain the crowd.

The unemployed young man accepted the offer since he needed money badly. He dressed up in his monkey suit and entertained the audience.

One day while he was entertaining as a monkey, he accidentally fell into the lion's cage.

Everyone was shocked watching the tense scene as the lion came closer to him but for some unknown reason didn't attack.

Instead, the lion came up very close to the monkey's face and whispered, "Joe, it's me, Frank. We had a digital calculus class together last year."

* When pilots fly aircraft and encounter equipment or aircraft problems, they are required to write up a report in the aircraft's maintenance log.

Then the aircraft maintenance engineer looks at the maintenance log and remedies the problem. Here are some humorous examples.

"Something is loose and jiggling in the cockpit."

Remedy: "Something was loose and tightened in the cockpit."

"Dead bugs splattered on the windshield."

Remedy: "Live bugs are on back-order."

"Autopilot set on hold altitude produces a 300 foot per minute descent.

Remedy: "Very sorry, I cannot reproduce problem on the ground."

"The friction locks are causing the throttle levers to be difficult to move and stick."

No remedy: "That's the purpose of what friction locks are for."

"The IFF (Identify Friend or Foe transponder) is inoperative."

Remedy: "Investigated thoroughly and found IFF inoperative in 'OFF' mode."

"There is a Mouse in cockpit."

Remedy: "Installed cat in cockpit."

"The number 3 engine missing."

Remedy: "After thorough search, Number 3 engine found on right wing."

* I am an engineer. To save us time, let's assume I am correct in everything I tell you.

* An engineer is a person who uses mathematics, physics, and other science disciplines to solve very difficult problems.

When there are no difficult problems to solve, engineers work very hard and steadily to make up new ones.

Entitlement

* There are people who have an unrealistic and illogical sense of being special or a feeling of entitlement. Although you may have heard otherwise, this will not give them a severe case of psychosis. They remain functional. But be aware they sincerely believe they can get any kind of sh*t they want, and they don't have to do anything for it.

* "Don't misunderstand me. I am a kind person and if I am kind that does not mean I'm weak or that you are entitled to more. If you think I am weak or treat me unkind, I guarantee you will not remember me as a weak person."

- Al Capone

Epitaphs

Here are a few interesting epitaphs from a few celebrity grave markers:

* A cowboy's epitaph,

"There were two things I loved in life, good horses and beautiful women. May they take this old hide of mine and make it into a lady's saddle, so I can rest in peace between two things I loved the most."

* "I won't be right back after this brief message."

- Merv Griffin

* "That's all folks."

    -Mel Blanc (Creator of Bugs Bunny)

* "I am ready to meet my Maker. Whether my Maker is ready for the immense tribulation of meeting with me is another concern."

    - Winston Churchill

* "There goes the neighborhood."

    - Rodney Dangerfield

* "And away we go!"

    - Jackie Gleason

* "I told you I was ill."

    - Spike Milligan

* Leslie Nielsen (Movie Actor in "Airplane", "Naked Gun", etc.) loved fart jokes and has on his tombstone: "Let 'er rip."

* "The best is yet to come."

- Frank Sinatra

Ethnic Humor

* "When I was in high school, I took French, so I joined the French club. We didn't do anything, we just sat there. Now and then, we'd surrender to the German club."

* Years ago, during the Bush era, Chris Rock joked, "You know the world is going crazy when the best rapper is a white guy, the best golfer is a black guy, the tallest guy in the NBA is Chinese, the Swiss hold the America's Cup, France is accusing the U.S. of arrogance, Germany doesn't want to go to war, and the three most powerful men in America are named "Bush", "Dick", and "Colin." Need I say more?"

    - Chris Rock

* Some of the initial training of astronauts took place on a Navajo reservation. A Navajo elder (who didn't speak English) and his son watched the training. The Navajo elder asked a young brave what they were doing in their fancy special suits.

He told him they were training for a trip to the moon. The elder got quite excited about that and asked to see if the astronauts would deliver a message for him.

NASA thought that would be excellent PR to involve Native Americans. So, they had the elder record his message in the Navajo language and the astronauts would carry the recording with them to the moon.

The elder recorded his message and NASA officials asked the young brave to translate it for them but he refused. NASA sent it to a US Government translator who reported the message simply read, "Watch out for these people. They will steal your land."

* A mother told her son, Joey, you should not be racist. Nope, don't be a racist. You should understand all people are equal, and you should not generalize or use stereotypes for anyone's ethnicity.

You should try to be like your friend Pasquale. He's Italian and he's a plumber. He doesn't follow you around like the old saying, "Wherever you go, dey go." He uses excellent plumbing parts made by Japanese people, and he speaks English even though he looks like a Mexican who installs floor tiles everywhere. He can jump just as high as a black man. And he earns tons of money like Jewish people.

* What's different between a black fairytale story and a white fairytale story?

White fairy tale stories begin with "Once upon a time..." Black fairy tale stories begin with "Y'all motherf*ckers ain't gonna believe dis sh*t!"

* "How many Mexicans are needed and how long does it take for them to build a -- Holy sh*t, they're finished!"

* Q: How do you know if there was a Chinese person in your house?

A. When you get home, you see your physics homework is done and completely correct. Your computer is cleaned, with all new updates are installed along with programs you didn't know would help you operate better. Also, if you look out the window you will still see the Chinese person still trying to back out into traffic from your driveway.

* A young German man got a job serving as a radioman in the US Coast Guard. He was fully trained to handle and relay any calls from ships in distress. On his first day of work, he got his first emergency call:

"Mayday! Mayday!"

"Oh, hallo! Vat ist happening?"

The radio crackles: "We're sinking! We're sinking!"

"Oh," the German radioman pauses. "Vat are you sinking about?"

* You know you're going to flunk a written exam when the Asian sitting next to you mumbles, "Sh*t!" when he first looks at the exam.

* Why are West Virginia redneck homicides so difficult to resolve?

A. All the DNA is the same and there are no dental records to check.

* From 1788 to 1868, Britain convicts were sent to the Australian colonies.

Recently, an American tourist arrived in Sydney and was being heavily interrogated by Australian immigration. His passport was in order, he declared everything he had to declare, but he kept being questioned.

After an hour of grueling questioning, he was asked again, "Have you ever been convicted of a crime?"

The tourist said, "Is that a requirement to enter Australia?"

* A man is shopping for a gift for a Mexican friend and noticed a Mexican bookstore.

He went into the bookstore and began to browse. He went through the shelves searching and then asked the clerk if he had any books about Donald Trump's foreign relations with Mexico.

The clerk replied, "Go to hell and get the f*ck out of here and don't come back."

"Yes, that's the one."

* During World War II, the Americans found it difficult to battle the Germans in trenches throughout Europe. Things seem to result in a stalemate.

The Americans devised a plan for the soldiers fighting in trenches. The Americans would call out, "Hans?" Then wait for a reply.

When the German stuck his head up and replied, "Ja!" he would be shot. This went on for days until the Germans figured out what was happening when they were losing a lot of soldiers.

So, the Germans devised their own plan. Their soldiers in trenches would call out, "Joe?"

But the Americans would shout back, "Is that you, Hans?"

"Ja!"

And the war in Europe started to turn favorably toward the Allies.

* Other children get intimidated by English children because they sound like they are 50 years old.

* There is more and more interracial dating going on now in fast-paced modern society since people of different cultures, different ethnic groups, different religions, are just simply looking for love and they don't have time to check if their colors match.

* "Everyone who is Italian is not in the Mafia," a young lady remarked. "My boyfriend is the typical Italian and I first thought he was in the Mafia, but he

assured me he wasn't. He finally asked me to marry him and gave me my ring, but I did have to take a finger out of it first."

* Religious researchers have proven Jesus was not Jewish but a black man. If you read the correct translation of John, Chapter 13, Verse 19, you will read Jesus was asked if he was the son of God. He ebonically replied, "I be He" in perfect American Black English.

Excuses

* Joe is going to gamble in Vegas but on his way to the casino his car breaks down. As he gets out of his car, a toad calls out, "You need a new fuel pump."

Joe, taken aback somewhat, calls road assistance and sure enough, he needed a new fuel pump. He is towed to a service station where he was told they had to order the part and it would be a day or two to get it. Then Joe hears the toad say, "Station across the street has one."

So, Joe goes across the street, and sure enough, they have the fuel pump and Joe is back on his way to the casino.

Joe says to the toad now sitting in his car, "You are some toad, eh?"

The toad replies, "Ribbit, some toad."

Joe decides to take the toad into the casino and puts it in his jacket pocket. Joe says, "Okay toad, now what?"

The toad says, "Ribbit. Roulette."

Joe asked the toad, "What do you think I should bet?"

The toad replies, "Ribbit. $20,000, red 7."

Even though the odds are slim, red 7 wins and Joe has a massive pile of chips.

Joe leaves with his chips and Joe takes his talking toad and gets the best suite in the hotel. He puts the toad down on the bed and says, "Toad, I don't know how you do it, but I want to help you since you won all this money for me."

The toad replies, "Ribbit, kiss me."

Joe thinks about it then says, "Why not?"

After he kisses the toad, the toad turns into a beautiful 17year-old girl.

"And that, your honor, is why this beautiful young girl was up in my room."

Failure

* When you forget about failures and treat it as water under the bridge, you are growing better and recovering from it. If you don't admit to failing, you are probably very stupid.

- Louis C. K.

* Joe is having a beer in a bar and his friend Harry walked in and slumped down next to him looking very depressed. "Harry, what's wrong?" Joe asked.

"Things aren't going well," Harry said.

"What happened?"

"I lost my job, I filed for bankruptcy, and I've got a family to feed."

"Harry, listen to me, no matter how bad things get, it can always get worse," Joe replied.

A week later, Harry walked into the bar and slumped down next to Joe.

"Harry! Great to see you. Are things going better for you now?"

"Hell no! My house burned down, I have no insurance, my wife and kids have left me, and my wife is divorcing me."

"Harry, no matter how bad things get, it can always get worse," Joe replied.

A week later, Harry walked into the bar and sat down next to Joe. "How's it going now, Harry?"

"Hell Joe, I just been to the doctor, and he's told me I've got terminal cancer."

"Well, no matter how bad things get, it can always get worse," Joe replied.

"Wait a minute, Joe. I'm not gonna let you keep telling me bullsh*t about things can always get worse. Every time you say the same thing: 'It can always get worse.' How the hell can things get worse, Joe?"

"Harry, all that sh*t could have happened to me."

* If you write a story about failures, and the book doesn't sell very well. Is the book a success?

- Jerry Seinfeld

* The good part of failing is that it's only temporary. The bad part about winning is that it's only temporary.

* Don't give up if you get a setback trying to reach your goal. Giving up with just one failure is like being in a boat trying to motor across a river then throwing your oars overboard because your engine breaks down.

* "Every failure is just an opportunity to learn something and start again, only this time wiser.

- Henry Ford

* Failure is not the opposite of success, it's part of success.

* The only person who hasn't failed at anything is the same person who didn't try anything.

- Theodore Roosevelt

* I've failed over and over again in my life and that is why I succeed.

- Michael Jordan

* I have not failed since I've found out several thousand ways that don't work.

- Thomas Edison

Family

* Our family was like an airport. Mom was the hub – the clearance area. You couldn't go around her or try to get anywhere nonstop.

She was the control tower and directed all the ground traffic taxiing for a takeoff. You had to wait to be cleared for takeoff or landing. Dad wasn't immune either, but he had more leeway than the rest of us.

- Will Schwalbe

* Joe's wife was on a business trip at a convention in Las Vegas that was poorly attended and a waste of time. Frustrated, she decided to shorten her trip and took the first flight out and arrived home late at night two days early.

She quietly put her bags down, took her shoes off, tip-toed upstairs, then very quietly opened the door to the bedroom.

As the door opened, the dim light from the hallway illuminated the bed. She became immediately enraged and shocked to see 4 legs under the covers instead of two!

She reached for a baseball bat in the corner of the bedroom and repeatedly slammed it into the bodies under the blanket as hard as she could. She disregarded the muffled groans and moans, wildly swinging the bat non-stop. Then she stomped out totally exhausted.

She staggered down the stairs and went into the den to pour herself a drink. As she entered the den, she saw her husband sitting there reading a book.

"Hi sweetheart!" He said. "Your parents have come to visit. They're using our bedroom. It's still early, so go up and say hello to them."

* "As a child I had a rare disease that required me to eat dirt three times a day. I'm very lucky my older brother told me about it."

- Milton Jones

* On his Birthday, Joe was mad because no one in his family or any so-called "friends" wished him a happy birthday.

As he walked into his office, his beautiful secretary Josephine said, "Good Morning Boss, and by the way Happy Birthday to you!"

Joe felt somewhat better knowing someone remembered. Then to Joe's surprise, Josephine said, "You're such a great boss, and it's your birthday, so I want to buy you lunch today.

They had lunch and Joe felt good about being remembered. Then to his surprise, Josephine said, "Joe, it's your birthday, why don't we go someplace. You should take the day off and I should too, and we should do something."

"Well, okay."

"My place is nearby, let's take a walk over there and I'll show you my place?"

Joe scratched his head. He was a married man and unsure whether this was a good idea. Then thought life is short so what the hell. "Okay," Joe said.

"Great! My place is just around the corner."

When they got to her place she said, "Take it easy Joe, relax and put your feet up. I'm going to get into something more comfortable in the bedroom. I'll be right back."

Joe knew this was his lucky day. "Fine!" Joe said.

She went into the bedroom and after a while, came out carrying a huge birthday cake. She was followed by his wife, his kids, dozens of his friends, and co-workers, all singing "Happy Birthday Joe" then stopped singing when they saw Joe sitting on the couch naked.

Farmers

* A police officer stopped at a farm one day. "I need to inspect your farm for illegally growing drugs."

The farmer replied, "Okay, but officer, please be sure you don't go in the field over there."

"What! You listen to me," said the officer, "I'm the police and I go wherever I want to on this place." The officer reached into his pocket and pulled out his badge and a search warrant and shoved it in the farmer's face.

"See this f*cking badge and warrant?! The badge and warrant mean I can go anywhere I wish! No questions asked. Do you understand?"

The farmer nodded.

Shortly thereafter, the Farmer heard loud screams. The police officer was running for his life chased by a mad bull. The bull was gaining ground and just as the bull was putting his head down to gore the terrified officer, the farmer yelled out, "Your badge! Show him your f*cking BADGE!"

* On a very small farm, a farmer lived with his wife, and they had three grown sons. They were not financially well off, in fact, they were very poor and just had a single cow on their small farm and depended on the cow for milk.

One morning, the wife of the farmer woke up early and checked on the cow and saw it was stone cold dead lying in the field with its four legs sticking up in the air. Knowing they couldn't afford milk; she became depressed and despondent and hung herself.

The farmer woke and saw his wife and cow dead. He became depressed and despondent and picked up his rifle and shot himself.

The first son got up and saw both of his parents were dead and saw the dead cow as well. He got very depressed and despondent and decided life was no longer worth living and went down to the river to drown himself. When he got there, he couldn't believe his eyes when he saw a mermaid sitting on the bank.

The mermaid said, "I'm a magical mermaid and I know what's happened. So, I will restore your parents and the cow if you have sex with me 5 times."

The son agreed but he couldn't have any more sex after four times, so the mermaid allowed him to drown himself in the river.

The second oldest son woke up and saw both his parents were dead and the cow was dead and became very depressed. He decided to go to the river to drown himself.

The magical mermaid was there and told him, "If you sex with me ten times, I will make everything right." The second son couldn't do any more than 6 times, so he drowned himself.

The youngest son woke and saw both his parents were dead. He became depressed and walked down to the river to end it all and saw the mermaid sitting there waiting for him.

"I am a magical mermaid. If you have sex with me 15 times I will make everything right in your life."

The son replied, "Fifteen times? Haha! Is that all? Why not twenty times in a row?"

The mermaid couldn't believe what she just heard.

But the young man continued. "Why not thirty times in a row?" The mermaid was speechless.

"Okay! Okay! If you have sex with me 30 times I will make everything right," said the mermaid.

"I'm not sure of that," said the young man. "Thirty times in a row might kill you like it did the cow."

Fast Thinking

* Very smart people have illegible handwriting because they think fast.

*An eccentric little old woman hadn't ever seen Africa and decided to take a trip there and took her little poodle along with her. They were out on a safari and the little poodle wandered off and got lost in dense jungle.

Trying to find his way back, the little poodle saw a huge lion rapidly approaching him.

The poodle starts to chew on bones on the ground and said as loud as he could, "Man that lion tasted great! Maybe I can find another lion to eat!"

Hearing this, the approaching lion ran away thinking "That was close! I was almost eaten by a poodle!"

A monkey saw all this going on and ran to tell the lion the poodle outsmarted him. The poodle saw the monkey running toward the lion but couldn't catch the monkey in time before the monkey told the lion the poodle made a fool out of him.

The angry lion told the monkey, "Hop on my back and watch me have that poodle for lunch."

The poodle saw the lion coming fast at him with a monkey on its back. The poodle yelled as loud as he could, "Where's that f*ckin' monkey. I sent him off some time ago to get another lion for me!"

* An old couple had just gone to sleep when the husband remembered he left the garage door open. Going out to close the door, he heard voices in the garage and suspected they were being robbed. He telephoned police.

He got through to the police station and said, "We're being robbed! There are intruders in our home! We need help!"

Dispatch told him to sit tight and leave the house since there weren't any more officers he could send out right then.

The old man waited then called back. "No need to send anyone. I just shot both the robbers and the dogs are having them for dinner."

As he hung up the phone, he heard several sirens in the distance. The robbers took off and the police arrested them as they fled.

An officer approached the old man. "You said you gunned down the robbers and your dogs were - "

The old man cut him off, "Yeah, and you said, for me to sit tight since there were no officers available to help?"

Father's Day

* When I was 14 years old, I thought my father was ignorant and I couldn't stand the old man. I was amazed however when I reached 21 at how intelligent my dad had become in just a few years.

- Mark Twain

* Joe bought a voice automated robot car that does anything he tells it to do correctly without any error.

Joe was very proud of what the car could do, and the car didn't make any mistakes.

One day, Joe was home, and his wife told him to tell the car to go and pick up the children from school. She was tired.

Joe agreed and said to the car: "Car, go and bring my children from school."

The car took off but didn't return as it usually does. Joe and his wife thought something must be wrong and both became concerned after several hours passed.

Joe was ready to call the police when he and his wife saw the car approaching overloaded with children.

The car parked right in front of them and said, "These are your children, sir."

Seated in the car were the neighbor's children, the schoolteacher's children, his wife's best friend's children, and his sister-in-law's children.

Joe's wife said, "Joe! Don't tell me all these are your children!"

Joe replied, "Can you first tell me why our children are not in the car?"

Fitness

* "It's great to stay in shape," said Ellen DeGeneres. "But not like my grandmother who started jogging at 60. She's 97 now and we don't really know where the hell she ran to."

Gambling

*One definition of a Lottery is a tax on people who are not very good at understanding the mathematics of chance and comparing odds.

* A Russian tourist named Boris visited Borneo and got lost in the jungle and was captured by natives. He was put in a cage and the natives went through his belongings and found a .38 revolver.

The natives hadn't ever seen a gun before and asked Boris to show them how the gun worked which he did. The natives were amazed, and Boris and the natives became good friends.

After a while, the natives grew bored just shooting the gun and Boris showed them how to play Russian Roulette. The natives loved it and played the game day after day and loved the excitement even though several natives lost at the game. Eventually, they let Boris go and he returned to Russia.

Years passed, and Boris returned to Borneo to visit the tribe to see how they were getting along. The chief of the village told Boris they had run out of bullets but had their own version of Russian Roulette and asked Boris if he wanted to play. Boris told them he would like to try the "Borneo version" of the game.

"Very well," the chief told him and called up six naked women. "Pick one, just anyone and she will give you a blowjob."

Boris scratched his head. "Chief, this looks like a lot of fun but where is the danger in this game?"

The chief smiled, "One of them is a cannibal."

* A nun wanted to enter the horse racing business but found out it was way too expensive for her, so she bought a little Mexican Burro.

She entered the Burro in the first race she could and without any formal training, it came in third place! But the horseracing news reported it as "Nun's Ass Chokes!"

The next day, however, she entered the burro into another race and won! The horseracing news reported it as, "Nun's Ass Wins Prize!"

On the next day, the burro wasn't himself, so the nun took it out of the race. The horseracing news reported it as, "Nun's Ass Scratched."

The nun decided to sell the burro cheaply to get rid of it and horseracing news reported, "Nun Sells Her Ass for $10."

Genius

* A university student failed his math class and asked his professor to change his grade. They discussed it back and forth and the student finally challenged him, "Sir, do you know everything about Math?

The professor replied, "Well I've been here at this University for 40 years and I believe I know a great deal about mathematics.

The student replied, "If you can answer one question, I won't bother you anymore and will accept my final mark. But, if you can't, you have to give me "A" Grade."

The math professor knew if brains were dynamite, this student couldn't blow his hat off, so the Professor agreed.

The student asked the professor, "Can you answer what is legal but not logical? But what is logical and not legal? And what is neither legal nor logical?"

The learned professor thought about it for hours but couldn't figure it out. He spent several days pondering about it. He reluctantly agreed to give the student an "A" but said he must first have the answer to this puzzling question.

The student replied, "Just ask the class."

The following day, the professor asked the class the same question and was shocked when the whole class raised their hands. He asked a student in the front of the class for the answer.

"Professor, you are 65, married to a 28-year-old woman. That is legal but not logical.

Your wife is having an affair with a 23-year-old student, this is logical but adultery, well it's not legal.

Your wife's boyfriend has failed his exam and yet you have agreed to give him an "A" Grade. This is neither logical nor legal.

*Two blind people started to argue, and they came very close to punching each other until I shouted, "Hey, you shouldn't fight, especially when I see one of you has a knife and other one doesn't." They both ran away.

* Every great genius must have some madness.

- Aristotle

* Looking back, the person who first created a hamburger was very creative and smart. But the person who first got the idea and later created the first cheeseburger was an absolute genius.

- Matthew McConaughey

Getting Even

* Joe lost all his money in Las Vegas and all he had left was his return airline ticket. He had to get to the airport. He waved down a cab. He told the cab driver he wanted to go to the airport.

The cab driver replied, "Oh you want to go to the airport. Hell, I was just going there without a passenger. You made my day. By the way, the fare is $25."

Joe said, "Look, I just lost everything I had on me, and I just need to get to the airport to return home. I'm good for the $25 and I'll send you $50 if you just drive me to the airport. Here, write down my I.D. information. I'm good for the $25."

But the cab driver refused. "Look, buddy, either you got $25 cash or get the hell out!" Joe left and hitchhiked to the airport and eventually made it home.

A month later, Joe returned to Vegas, but this time he won a lot of money. As he was leaving for the airport, he noticed the cab driver who refused to take him to the airport the last time when he had no money was sitting at the end of a long cab line. There were 20 cabs in front of him.

Joe decided to get even and have some fun. He got into the first cab in the line and said, "How much to take me to the airport?"

"$25 dollars," said the first cab driver in line.

Joe continued, "And how much to give me a blowjob on the way to the airport?"

The first cab driver told Joe to get the hell out of his cab.

So, Joe got in the next cab and asked the same two questions, and so on and all drivers refused until Joe got to the last cab.

When Joe got in the cab of the driver who refused to take him last year when he had no money, he said, "How much to take me to the airport?"

"$25," said the cab driver. "But why did those other drivers not take you?"

"I really don't know, they just said, they didn't want to go to the airport. Hey, here's $25 in advance. By the way, drive slowly by these drivers in line, so I can show them you were the one who is taking me to the airport?

The cab driver did this and as they passed the other cab drivers in line, Joe rolled down his window and smiled at every driver giving a thumbs up.

Golf

* Lee Trevino came from a poor background and sometimes ran into a racist remark. He mentioned when he was a kid caddying, the lighter colored Hispanics got more caddying jobs than he and his other friends did. But Lee was blessed with an amazing sense of humor.

From his great success on the PGA Tour, he and his wife were able to buy a very nice home.

One day, he was cutting his lawn out in front of his beautiful home, when an older woman stopped her Cadillac at the curb and lowered the window.

"Sir, do you speak English?" She asked.

"Why, yes I do," Lee answered.

"How much are they paying you for your working here?" She asked.

Lee smiled and said, "Oh, I don't get paid, but the lady of the house lets me sleep with her."

* There are similarities between a mountain climber and a very bad golfer. The bad golfer goes, "Whack! - Sh*t!" The mountain climber goes, "Shit! - Whack!"

* A very good young golfer played in a local tournament and was followed around the course by an older woman totally enamored with him.

She waited around until after the round and went up and told him how much she admired him and his play and his shooting three under par for a 69 that day. She offered to take him home for dinner which he accepted.

"A 69! It was great to watch such a handsome man like you play and you're only 21 years old! You've got a great career in front of you," she said over dinner.

"Yeah, I don't shoot a 69 very often on that course," he politely replied.

The woman gave him a wink and said, "How about you and I do a 69?"

The young man, a bit inexperienced, asked,

"What's a 69?"

"Well, you put your head between my legs, and I put my head between your legs."

The young man accepted, and they took off their clothes but just as he put his head between her legs, she let out a roaring fart.

"Oh! I'm so sorry, please excuse me," she laughed and laughed.

The young man nodded then tried to put his head between her legs and again she let out another roaring fart right in his face. "Oh! Sorry again," she said.

The young man got up and got dressed and walked out saying, "I'm not doing that another 67 times."

   * Practical Joke. If one of your regular group has bought a brand-new super driver and has let everyone on earth know about it (especially if he

bought it on sale), there's an old well-known prank that still brings a lot of laughs.

Take an old wooden scratched driver – the most hideous one you come across (perhaps the pro shop might have an old, decrepit driver in the back – one with cobwebs on it in the Lost and Found Bin), and while your braggart friend with the new driver is distracted, or, in the toilet, etc., take the brand-new head cover off his new driver, and put the new head cover on the decrepit driver and stick it in his bag.

Carefully hide his new driver under another head cover in his own bag or your bag or wherever you can keep it absolutely safe. Have a good laugh when he discovers it.

* Serious golfers? No, we aren't serious when we play golf. We ride around in a golf cart getting drunk and we don't let playing golf get in the way of our drinking.

* After finishing their round on the Old Course at St. Andrews, 4 golfers went up to the bar on the top floor of a hotel overlooking the course for refreshments.

They sat down at a table and decided to do a 7-whiskey tasting ranging from very smooth scotches (which go down as easy as a glass of water), to smoky, peaty scotches. After tasting 7 whiskeys, they were all well-oiled.

One of the guys got up and walked around to the bar, then noticed a locked cabinet with iron bars and complex combination locks. Surveillance cameras hanging from the ceiling were positioned on it. The guy said, "Bartender, what's in that cabinet?"

"That, my dear sir, is an extremely rare bottle of scotch known as the infamous, "Esmeralda's Islay". It's on loan to us for a few days. There are none better."

"Can I see it?" asked the guy.

The bartender paused, then motioned to a uniformed guard wearing white gloves who opened the cabinet and brought out the beautiful bottle on its elaborate display stand.

The guy bent over to get a closer look at it and let out a fart. The guy nervously glanced around to see if anyone noticed his fart, but the bartender and guard were total professionals and acted like nothing happened.

Embarrassed, the guy moved to another seat pretending to get a better view of the beautiful English Crystal Decanter covered in gold and diamonds. Then says, "How much is it?"

The bartender replied, "My good sir, if you farted just looking at it, you're going to shit yourself when I tell you the price."

Golf Rules

* No matter how you play, you will lose the match to the golfer in your foursome who annoys you the most.

* When playing through another foursome who allow you to play through on a par three, the first in your group will lose his golf ball in thick bush.

The second will slice terribly and nearly hit the players who allowed your group to play through.

The third off the tee will snap hook his shot and narrowly miss players on an adjacent tee box.

The fourth will hit it two feet from the pin.

* Thinking your golf play cannot get any worse is a definite sign that your golf play will get worse.

* If you are 180 yards away from a green which is almost surrounded by deep bunkers except for a very narrow 3-yard-wide center patch of clear apron, you should aim directly at the deep bunker on the far-left side of the green and your ball will automatically roll up to the center of the green.

* If you hit a brand-new ball which barely rolls into a water hazard, keep your eyes on the exact spot your ball rolled in and you will find 4 old, yellowed golf balls some with cut covers, but you won't find your new ball.

* When you try out a new driver inside a major golf retailer, the sound effects in the indoor tryout range will sound exactly like a PGA Tour Golfer hit it. When you take it to the course and hit your first drive, it will sound like your new driver is made from cracked bamboo.

* A foursome was out playing a golf course with a par three hole with a volcano right by it.

But only three of them finished the round. The club pro came out and asked where Harry was?

One of them sadly said, "He hit it close to the crater. Suddenly, we heard sounds like heavy seas swishing and crashing against the rocks, then a great rumble, then the ground shook, then we heard a great hissing sound, then a large boulder as big as a pickup truck came shooting out of the crater about 100 feet high right above Harry."

"Didn't he get out of the way," the club pro asked?

"He looked up at the boulder…ah, his last words were, 'What the f*ck?'… then the boulder came down and flattened him like a cue ball hitting a bowl of oatmeal."

"Sh*t! I'll get out there right away," the pro said!

"Don't bother, we don't need a ruling - we're just playing socially, and by the way, the boulder sent his ball flying on the green and into the hole and we already gave him a courtesy birdie in our match."

* If you are unfortunate enough to accidentally hit into a group of women golfers in front of you, the following will automatically occur:

- The pro shop will be called.

- The course marshal will immediately be seen beelining directly toward you.

- The rest of your foursome will be pointing at you when the women turn around to see who hit the shot.

- No matter how much you apologize, know that you will be stalked for the rest of your round for every shot you hit until you finish.

- When you are trying to relax in the clubhouse, strange women will be pointing at you saying, "There he is."

- Your car will have all windows broken and 4 flat tires when you return to it.

- Your dog will bite you when you get home.

Heaven

* Can you imagine what would happen if you found out when you died that there is no heaven and or hell, but we all went to the same place?

In other words, no matter how you lived your life, we would all go to the same place?

There would be a lot of very nice people really upset. Can you imagine seeing Billy Graham and Mother Theresa angry as hell and arguing with the gate keeper saying, "What is this sh*t!"

* A woman in her mid-sixties had a heart attack and went to heaven. She didn't want to die and pleaded with God to send her back to Earth and give her more time. The Good Lord conceded and agreed to 15 more years.

Suddenly she woke up in the hospital. She thought, "While I'm here I might as well get some other things done. So, she got a makeover including a facelift, a tummy tuck, and breast augmentation.

As she left the hospital she was struck and killed when a bus ran over her. When she met with God again, she was very upset. "God! What the hell? What the hell happened? I thought you said I had more time on earth! Don't you remember you gave me '15 more years?'"

"Oh sh*t! That was you? I'm very sorry. I couldn't tell that was you."

　　* A bold adventurer went into a dark African jungle when he saw a band of machete bearing warriors approaching so he climbed a tree. He watched them from above as they were chopping off the heads, arms and legs, or other parts of anyone in their way.

Suddenly the limb he was standing on started to crack and break. A few of the warriors looked up and spotted him and started to climb the tree after him.

He began to pray, "Lord help me, I am doomed! I am totally fucked."

Suddenly, the clouds opened, and a ray of sunshine beamed down, and a loud voice boomed out, "No, you are not doomed. Jump to the ground and pick up that large rock at your feet and bash in the head of the biggest warrior."

So, the adventurer leaped to the ground, picked up the rock and smashed the head of the biggest warrior. The rest of the warriors started to back off.

The adventurer laughed and kicked the body of the large warrior. Then he taunted any other warrior to get near him and to his dismay, they began to close in on him!

The same voice boomed out of the heavens again. "Now, you are definitely f*cked."

* Music speaks of a "Stairway to Heaven" and a "Highway to Hell." That may be an indication where the traffic is going.

* A large bus full of nuns were killed in a crash and the next thing they know they are all facing the Pearly Gates waiting for St. Peter.

St. Peter greets them. "Sisters, welcome to heaven. But before I can let you in, I must ask you each a question. Please line up in single file."

St. Peter asks the first nun, "Have you ever touched a man's private parts?"

"Well... there was only one time... but just barely touched one with my little finger."

St. Peter said, "Fine. Place the finger you touched the penis within the Holy Water. After that, you may go through to Heaven."

St. Peter asked the second nun in line, "How about you sister, have you touched a penis?"

"Only once, I held one in my hand for just a second."

"Fine, sister, please wash that hand in the Holy Water and then go through the pearly gates."

St. Peter heard a commotion in line. A nun was trying to get ahead of another nun in line. St. Peter said, "Sister Josephine, what's wrong? There's no rush!"

Sister Josephine said, "Well I've got to gargle that Holy Water and I want to do it before Sister Gertrude put her ass in it."

* Mother Teresa and God were sitting down together for a meal of simple bread and soup in heaven.

Mother Teresa looked at the meal and then looked down into hell where the damned were enjoying a lavish feast and was confused but didn't say anything.

The next evening the same scenario, bread and soup in heaven, a huge feast in hell.

The third evening Mother Teresa had to say something, "God, I'm not complaining, but I wonder about what I am seeing? Why do we have only bread and soup but the people in hell are enjoying an amazing feast?

God replied, "Well you know, Teresa, it doesn't pay to cook for two."

* A good man died and was up before the pearly gate's judgment. He was met by St. Peter who greeted him. "Sir, you were a good man but before you meet God, I thought I should tell you that other than you're being a good man, you really didn't do

anything outstanding for the common good, or for the bad, so we're not sure what to do with you. What particularly did you do on earth that was outstanding?

The good man pondered for a bit and said, "Once in California, I was driving back to the hotel and there in the parking lot, I saw a young woman being tormented by a group from a Motorcycle Gang – you know revving their engines, circling her, taunting her with obscenities?"

"Go on," said St. Peter.

"So, I stopped and got out of my car with a tire iron went up to the leader – the biggest guy there. He was much bigger than I, very muscular, had tattoos all over, a scar on his face and a ring in his nose. "Well, I put my index finger in his nose ring and tore it out of his nose. Then I told him and the rest of them they'd better stop bothering this woman or they all would get more of the same!"

"Wow, that's very impressive sir!" St Peter replied. "When did you do this?"

"Just a little while ago."

* John staggered in the door late in the evening after an afternoon round of golf followed by several beers, then a big spicy dinner at a Mexican Restaurant, with 5 Tequilas and 7 Coronas to wash it all down.

"I'm bushed honey, I'm going to bed early," Joe said to his wife. Joe went to sleep but woke up and saw a white-haired man in white flowing robes standing at the end of his bed.

"What the hell? Who are you? How did you get in here?" Joe said.

"This isn't your bedroom, Joe. I'm St. Peter and you are at the Pearly Gates."

"What! I'm dead? I'm too young to die! Send me back right now!"

"Sorry Joe, it's not that easy. We don't usually send them back, but I can send you back as a cat or a hen. It's your choice," St. Peter said.

Joe didn't like cats, and being a hen didn't seem that great either, but it was his only other choice.

"Okay, I'll go back as a hen," said Joe.

Instantly, Joe is on a farm walking around with other hens on a bright sunny day. He liked the sunshine and nice weather and is enjoying himself.

A rooster walked up to him and said, "You must be the new hen St. Peter told me about. How do you like being a chicken?"

"Well, it's okay, but I feel like my ass is about to explode."

"Oh, that's just the ovulation going on, you've got to lay an egg," said the rooster.

"Okay," says Joe, "How do I lay an egg?"

"Well, when you feel it coming on, let out a cluck and push."

Joe clucked and pushed. An amazing egg comes out!

"Hey that felt really great," Joe said to the rooster.

Joe felt the urge again, pushed, and another egg popped out!

He did it again, and then heard his wife shouting, "Joe! Wake up! You're sh*tting in the bed!

* A poor beggar dies and stands before the pearly gates. Saint Peter greets him and says, "Welcome, poor soul. We have a special bonus for people like you because your life was exceptionally difficult. You can have a private audience with anyone you want to who is here in heaven and ask any question you want. Are you interested?"

The poor man considers what he has just heard. He rubs his chin in thought, then says, "Why yes, there is someone I would like to ask a question. Could I ask the Virgin Mary a question?"

Saint Peter answers, "No problem. I will arrange the meeting."

Shortly thereafter the poor man is alone in a room with Mary. He timidly and humbly asks his question. "Mary, in all the statues and paintings I saw of you on Earth, you always looked a little sad. Why is that?"

Mary looks left and right to be sure no one is listening. In a hushed whisper, she confides, "I always wanted a girl."

Horses

* A cowboy who was an expert horseman, and his girlfriend got married and went down the road to the hotel in their small redneck town on their honeymoon night. The cowboy went in to get a room and told the clerk this was a very important evening, and he wanted the best room they have.

"The clerk said, "Well, I can give you the bridal?"

"No, not needed," said the cowboy. "I'll just hold on to her hair and ears until she gets used to it."

* A 66-year old man was born on June 6th and was married to his 6th wife for 6 years. He earned $66,666.66 every 6 months. Six was his lucky number.

He learned there was a horse named "Lucky Devil 666" running in the 6th race at the racetrack 6 miles from his home on 6th street.

He took out $66,666.66 from his bank account and bet it all on the horse to win.

Sure enough, the horse came in 6th.

Hospitals

* A very beautiful woman was covered with a sheet as she was being taken down the hospital corridor for a small operation on her leg. The staff member taking her said, "I'll put you here against the wall and I'll go in to see if there is a wait before your surgery."

A young man in a white coat walked over to the cart the woman was lying on and raised up the sheet. He paused, then continued down the hallway.

The same thing happened again, he went by, lifted the sheet, then walked away.

A short while later, the young man came by and lifted the sheet and the young woman asked, "Doctor, am I going to have my surgery soon?"

The young man said, "Don't ask me, I just fill the concession machines."

* A woman was running down the hall with only her hospital gown on before she was about to

be operated on. A guard stopped her and asked her what was going on?

"Well, the nurse was saying, 'This will be a very simple operation. Don't worry so much about it even though it's the first time.'"

The guard said, "The nurse was just trying to make you relax and not be nervous about the operation."

"But she wasn't saying that to me. She was saying that to the young doctor!"

Insanity

* I may be insane, but it does not trouble me as I enjoy every minute of it.

- Edgar Allan Poe

* Believing that you are insane is a good sign you are sane.

* A boy called a police station, and the desk sergeant answered the phone. The boy said, "Hello, I was wondering if you might have a gun?"

The sergeant replied, "Yes."

"Then shove it up your ass!" Then the boy hung up.

The sergeant called back, and a woman answered. "Hello?"

"Your boy just called! He told me to shove my gun up my ass!"

"Oh, really? Well, how long ago did he call?"

"About 2-3 minutes ago." The sergeant said.

"Well, you don't have to call here to find out what to do. You should know better than to take a little boy so seriously. You can take the gun out of your ass now."

* Statistics clearly show one in four people have some type of mental illness. If you carefully study three people you know very well and if you conclude they are fine, then it's you.

- Rita Mae Brown

Irony

   * Always remember that you are a one and only person. There is no one else who was ever like you - just like everyone else."

   -Margaret Mead

   * A very sad guy sat at a bar staring at his drink. He stared at this drink for half of an hour.

A huge trouble-maker big and burly guy sat down next to him, took the drink from the sad guy, and downed it all in one gulp.

The sad guy started crying – sobbing away uncontrollably.

The big guy said, "Hey, Sorry, man. I was just f*ckin' around. Hey! I'll buy you another one."

"No, it's not that. This day has been terrible – the worst ever in my entire life. First, I slept too long and got in late to the office. My boss, who never liked me anyway, somehow thought coming in late was a federal crime and totally outrageous and fired me!

The sad guy continued, "When I left the building, I couldn't find my car and found out it was stolen. The police said my car was probably being stripped for parts – I won't get it back and I've got no insurance. Then I get a cab to go home, and when I leave the cab, I must have left my wallet and credit cards in the back seat. So, I ran after the cab, but the cab driver just drove away."

The sad guy went on. "I go into my house, and I find my wife in bed with my neighbor, and my wife yelled at me and told me to get out and she will be filing for divorce. So, I leave the house and come to this bar. And just when I was thinking about putting an end to my life, you show up and drink my poison."

* My family and friend laughed like hell at me when I told them I was going to be a comedian. Haha! They're not laughing now.

- Bob Monkhouse

* I hate people who use big words just to impress other people with their sesquipedalian loquaciousness.

* I think my neighbor is peeper and watching me. She's also investigating me. I'm sure of this and know this as a fact. She's been googling my name and address. I saw her through my binoculars to see what she does every night.

* There are four types of people, those who can do the math and those who can't.

* "Why is 'abbreviation' such a long word?"

– George Carlin

Judo

* Being funny in life doesn't take a lot of energy and it's quick and efficient - like Judo.

- Jon Stewart

* Joe competed in a Judo contest and made it to the final round. But Joe's final opponent was much quicker than Joe. He was the world-renowned Sunny Chopsticks, an 11th-degree Juichidan Black Belt known for his famous and inescapable "Octopuso" submission hold. No one has ever got out of that hold.

The match began, and Sunny Chopsticks got the advantage over Joe and put him into the Octopuso hold.

Suddenly, there is a blood-curdling scream and Sunny Chopsticks went flying 6 feet in the air and then hit the mat so hard he knocked himself out. Joe pinned him for the win.

A reporter asked Joe, "How did you get out of the Octopuso?"

"Well, I knew I was dead meat when he got me in that hold. I opened my eyes and through the blur, I could see these big pink testicles.

So, I stretched my neck with all my might, and I bit down on those babies just as hard as I could. It was amazing how much strength one has when you bite your own balls!"

Jumping to Conclusions

* Joe and his fiancé got married. Joe loved his new bride very much, but when they returned from their honeymoon, they weren't talking to each other. Not one bit.

Joe went to work after he returned and was approached by his boss, "Hey Joe, how did the honeymoon go?"

"Okay at first, but I was single for a while after my divorce, and I wasn't getting used to married life just yet."

"What do you mean 'Not used to it,'" his boss asked?

"After we finished having sex, I put a $100 bill on the pillow – it was just habit, and I didn't think twice about it."

"Wow! You are in in trouble, Joe! Maybe your wife will feel better with time?"

"Hell, I don't care how she feels. The problem I have is she left $80 change!"

* Frank Sinatra asked me to accompany him to the premiere debut of "The Detective." People always jump to conclusions. He was a perfect gentleman and very protective towards me. There was no sex involved.

- Jacqueline Bisset

* When companies are successful or when they are not successful, they almost immediately jump to the wrong conclusions about how they got there or why they didn't get there.

- Ed Catmull, American Computer Scientist and President of Pixar

* Don't jump to conclusions. A good judge won't be always liking the conclusion he reaches. If a judge liked every conclusion, the judge is possibly doing something wrong.

- Antonin Scalia, Retired Associate Justice of the US Supreme Court

Lawyers

* The best lawyer is a brilliant, effective, and persuasive salesman.

- Janet Reno, Former US Attorney General

* A lawyer dies and goes to heaven. When he arrives at the pearly gates, there is a long line of good people waiting to go through the pearly gates.

The lawyer goes to the back of the long line. Just then the lawyer hears St. Peter call out, "Hey God! Let the word spread throughout heaven to have everyone come here!"

Suddenly a thousand angels appear, saints appear, Mother Theresa herself comes marching out with open arms and a big smile on her face.

They all pick up the lawyer and carry him through the gates. The others in line are talking amongst themselves and are annoyed at all the commotion.

St. Peter announces to the people in line, "Hey! Don't be mad. You'll all get it Heaven. Lord almighty, What a day! We just haven't had a lawyer up here for a while."

* Why have scientists begun using lawyers instead of rats for experiments? A. The scientists don't become fond or attached to the rats.

* Sam is on his deathbed and his 30-year law partner, Joe, visits him.

Sam announces, "Joe, I have to make a confession to you. I've been stealing from you for the past 15 years, and I've been having an affair with your wife for the past 20 years. I am the father of your son."

"Sam don't worry about that, and don't give it any thought at all. Oh, by the way, I'm the guy who put strychnine in your coffee."

* Two very old, retired lawyers went golfing and both severely sliced their drives. They were deep in the rough searching for their errant tee shots. Neither of them wanted to lose a new ball so they searched and searched and eventually wandered off the golf course and came upon a pair of tracks.

They stopped and examined the tracks closely. The first old lawyer announced, "My ball hit these tracks and probably rolled down this way somewhere and I'm going to follow these tracks."

The second old lawyer responded, "Our golf balls couldn't possibly go that way down these tracks – at least not very far. I'm not going to waste my time or this golf round searching for your f*cking ball in that direction. Besides any idiot could easily see by looking at the level of the land, our balls probably went the other way!"

Each old attorney believed himself to have the superior analysis of the situation, and they both bitterly argued on and on. Neither of them would back off from their argument, and they were still arguing heavily when the train hit them.

* After years of being single, a previously confirmed bachelor decided to take a wife and got engaged to a very beautiful woman. Instead of a huge wedding, they decided to elope.

They packed their suitcases and were so excited about driving to the chapel the bachelor drove erratically and crashed his car into a tree killing them both.

They woke up finding themselves in front of the Pearly Gates. It took them a bit, but after a while, they realized they must be dead.

While waiting for St. Peter to open the gates, they wondered whether they could get married in heaven by a Catholic priest.

Then the huge pearly gates began to slowly open as St. Peter walked out and approached them with his laptop in hand.

"St. Peter," the bachelor said, "We were wondering if we could get married in heaven?" The bachelor told St. Peter what had just happened with their unfortunate car crash.

St. Peter shook his head, "I don't think we've ever had two people get married in heaven? Wait here, I'll check."

St. Peter went back inside and closed the gates. Weeks passed. Long lines of people waiting to get into heaven started to form. St Peter was nowhere to be found.

The bachelor and his fiancé wondered what was going on. They start to have second thoughts about getting married, thinking they might not get along in the eternity ahead and they could have problems with their relationship now that they were going into heaven. They wondered if divorce was allowed in heaven.

Finally, after 10 weeks passed, the gates opened, and St. Peter walked out holding his laptop. He was smiling, but he looked very tired and worn out.

"Yep, I'm happy to say, we can arrange for you to get married in Heaven," St. Peter said.

"That's wonderful!" The bachelor said. "But St. Peter, ah…, while we were waiting, we wondered if our marriage didn't work out, could we get divorced in heaven?"

St Peter looked at the long line of people waiting and started to get angry. He shook his head and walked around in circles a bit, and then said, "Oh Hell! Are you f*cking with me?"

"No, we're not. Why are you so angry?" The bachelor said.

St. Peter opened his laptop and checked on somethings. But as he checked he grew angrier. Trying very hard to control his anger, he kept muttering to himself, "You two are f*cking with me, aren't you?"

"No. We're just asking," the bachelor said.

St Peter slammed his laptop down on a cloud and said, "It took me 10 weeks to find a Catholic priest up here. I'm not going to spend my time trying to find a lawyer."

* A lawyer just lost a career making case, so Satan sees this as an opportunity to approach him and make him an offer.

Satan: "I will make you the most successful lawyer in history. You will never lose a case again. You will be famous. You will be wealthy beyond your wildest imagination."

Lawyer: "What's the catch?"

Satan: "I want the souls of your parents, your siblings, your spouse, your children and all your future descendants for damnation in hell for all eternity."

Lawyer: "Okay, but what's the catch?"

* Three lawyers, Phillips, Johnson, and Henderson were sitting around the office playing poker. Johnson lays down a Royal Flush.

"I win!" said Johnson.

Henderson stands up and throws his cards on the table. "That's it, I've had it! Johnson is cheating."

Phillips asks, "What are you talking about? How do you know he's cheating?"

Henderson says, "Sh*t, he's cheating since those are the same cards I just dealt him."

* To get into heaven, a mathematician, a physicist, and a lawyer are all asked the question of what is the sum of 2+2?

The mathematician answered: "4"

The physicist answered: "Something between 3.95 and 4.05"

The lawyer closed the door, made sure that no one was listening, and then asked, "Which answer would you like to hear?"

Live in the Moment

* Don't be concerned with the future. Live in the moment. I don't consider the future since it will be here soon enough.

- Albert Einstein

Marital Bliss

* Joe said someone stole his credit card, but he didn't report it since whoever stole his credit card was spending less than his wife.

* Joe was a model husband. He worked long hours for a large accounting firm trying to make partner and get as much business and revenue as he could for the firm. Trying to stay fit, Joe religiously went to the gym two nights a week, and he plays golf every Saturday.

His wife of two years was happy he was such a determined man, but she wanted him to relax more. She decided to surprise him and take for his birthday to a local Strip Club one evening. When they drove up, the parking valet at the Club opened the door for Joe's wife. He then went around and took the keys from Joe.

"Nice to see you again, Joe." The parking valet said.

His wife wondered, "Joe, have you been here before?"

"No, haven't ever been here. That guy goes to the same gym I do."

They get a table up front, and the waitress brings Joe a bourbon and water. "Here's your usual Joe, what would your guest like to drink?"

Joe's wife orders a wine, then says, "How did she know you like bourbon and water?"

"She's a bartender at the golf course and knows that's what I drink, sweetheart."

A dancer comes up to their table and rubs her breasts in Joe's face while mussing his hair with both hands and says, "Hi Joey, you want your usual lap dance tonight?"

Joe's wife is fuming and grabs her purse and storms out the door. She waves a taxi down outside. Joe follows her and just gets into the taxi before his wife can slam the door on him. Joe begins pleading with his wife explaining the dancer must have mistaken him for someone else. He begs her to understand. Joe's wife is going bezerk, yelling at him non-stop. She's using every four-letter expletive known to man. Joe continues pleading when the taxi driver turns around and says, "You picked up a real bitch this time, Joe."

* A disgruntled wife went to see a psychic. The room was dark and hazy as the psychic peered into a crystal ball, studying it very closely.

The psychic slowly looked up and said, "This reading has some very bad news for you, I'm afraid."

"Just tell me," Dorothy said nervously.

"Alright, there's isn't any nice way to tell you this, Dorothy, so, I'll just be blunt…prepare yourself to be a widower."

"A widower? Really?"

"Your husband will die a violent, horrible, and excruciating death this year."

Visibly shaken, Dorothy stared at the psychic's lined face, then at the single flickering candle, then down at her hands.

Dorothy took a few deep breaths trying to compose herself.

Dorothy started to ask the psychic something, then hesitated, then realized she simply had to know.

She stared at the psychic for several minutes in silence without blinking. She gathered he courage and asked:

"Will they catch me?"

* Joe is home, and his wife is at the front door shouting at him to open the door. "Joe! Open the

f*cking door! It's raining out here! I'm getting drenched!"

At the same time, Joe's dog, "Bullshit" is at the backdoor barking and growling his head off.

So, who does Joe let in first?

Joe lets Bullshit in first since he'll shut up after Joe lets him in.

* Joe just left work early and went to the gym and finished working out much earlier than he expected and decided to call to let his wife know he'd be home early. A woman answered. Joe didn't know who she was and said, "Who's this?"

"I'm the maid," she answered.

"But, we don't have any maid?"

"My name is Maria. I was employed early today by the lady."

"Oh hi! I'm the lady's husband. Nice to talk with you. Can you tell her I'm on the phone?"

"Oh, she's upstairs in the bedroom with a man who I think is her husband."

"What!" Joe is fuming. He thinks back on how his wife wasn't expecting him until much later and she was in such a rush to get him out of the house this morning.

Joe said, "Listen, Listen Maria, would you like to make $25,000?"

"Si Senor! What do you want me to do?"

"Get the rifle out of the den, then quietly go upstairs and shoot them both!"

Maria puts the phone down and Joe hears her go upstairs, then he hears gun blasts.

Maria returns. "What do you want me to do with their bodies?"

"Put the bodies in the shed in the yard outside and I'll get rid of them later," Joe said.

"There's no shed out in the yard."

"Uh...is this 555-1127?"

* A Swiss, an Italian and a Frenchman were seated next to each other on a flight. After a few drinks, they started discussing their sex lives.

"Last night I made love to my wife four times," the Swiss said and this morning she made me delicious breakfast and she told me how much she adored me."

"Ah, last night I made love to my wife six times," the Italian said, "and this morning she made me a wonderful omelet and told me she could never love another man."

The Frenchman remained silent until he was asked, "And how many times did you make love to your wife last night?"

"Once," he replied.

"Only once?" the Italian arrogantly asked. "And what did she say to you this morning?"

"Don't stop," replied the Frenchman.

* After weeks of suspicion, Dorothy, a very jealous wife whose husband always seemed to be working late, fired their very attractive maid.

As the beautiful maid was leaving, she said, "Your husband told me that I'm a better housekeeper than you are."

The jealous wife shrugged her indifference.

"I'm also better in the sack," said the maid.

"My husband told you that?"

"No, the gardener did."

* Bob, went on a camping trip deep in the forest with his wife, kids, and mother-in-law.

One evening, just before going to bed for the night, Bob's wife looked around and realized her mother is gone.

Rushing to her husband, she insisted they both go and search for her mother right away.

Bob picked up his shotgun and gave his wife a rifle and went out to search for her. They eventually find her backed up against a tree and a large Grizzly bear is standing up facing her and growling ferociously.

Bob's wife says, "Do something!"

Bob studies the drama and watches his mother-in-law start to kick the bear in the groin and the bear is doubling over. "Sh*t! I'm not doing a damn thing.

That stupid bear got himself into this, so he's got to get out of it himself!"

* Joe and his wife, Jane, were celebrating their wedding anniversary at a very nice restaurant.

"Jane, I was wondering if you ever were unfaithful to me over the years," Joe said.

"Oh, Joe, I don't want to talk about…"

"Jane, I really want to know."

"Oh, all right. Three times."

"Three? Okay, when were they," asked Joe?

"Well Joe, remember when we first got married you really needed a loan, and no bank would touch you? Well, remember the chief bank loan officer came over to the house with a check for you and had you sign all the loan papers?"

"Oh, Jane, you did that for me? I think even more of you now…but when was the second time?"

"Remember when you had your heart attack and were close to death? No one wanted to do the heart surgery on you. Then the best cardiac surgeon in town suddenly appeared and operated on you?"

"Oh, gosh Jane, I love you very much. You saved me from dying. So, when was the third time?"

"Well, Joe, remember last year when you wanted to be the Golf Club Captain and you were 27 votes short?"

* An efficiency expert told his audience he loved the efficiency field since everywhere he looked he saw where things could be done quicker and easier because of his expertise.

"I studied my wife's routine at breakfast for years. She went back and forth between the stove, refrigerator, table, and cabinets just carrying one thing at a time.

So, I told her, "You're wasting time. Why don't you try carrying several things at once?"

A member in the audience asked if carrying several things at a time worked better.

"Why yes, it did. It used to take my wife 20 minutes to cook breakfast. Now I do it in ten."

* Wives are more dangerous than armed robbers. That's because gunmen want either your money or your life, while wives want both.

* A husband and wife are sitting at home in the evening watching television.

The husband is drinking a glass of his favorite beer and the wife is drinking a glass of her favorite wine. "I love you," says the husband.

Surprised, the wife says, "Is that you or the beer talking?"

"This is me talking to the beer."

*Several guys in the gym locker room are getting dressed when a mobile phone on a bench begins to ring. Joe picked it up and answered it.

"Hello?"

"Hi Luv, it's me are you still at the gymnasium?"

"Why yes I am," said Joe.

"I'm at the mall and found this beautiful coat. It's only $1,500 and I want to buy it. Is it okay?

"Sure, go ahead if you really like it," Joe said.

"I stopped at the Jaguar dealership, and they've got a brand-new XF Model in and I really like it."

"How much is it?"

"$70,000."

"Well okay buy it but make sure you get all the options," Joe said.

"Great! Oh, by the way, the home on the lake we were looking at had its price dropped the price to $2.1 million."

"Well go ahead and offer $2,050,000 and see if they take it. If not give them full price," Joe suggested.

"That's great! I will do that! Love you, honey. You are the best!

"Well, you're worth every penny. Love you too. Bye."

Joe hangs up. The other guys in the locker room are staring at him speechless.

Joe says, "Anybody know whose phone this is?"

* Scientists received a grant to study the difference between genders in being overweight. After months of research, it was found that women who are just slightly overweight live longer than men who mention it.

* Joe's wife was preparing their usual soft-boiled eggs and toast for breakfast, wearing only the tee shirt she normally slept in. Joe walked in and she softly said to Joe, "You've got to make love to me this very instant."

Joe thought he must still be dreaming, or this was his lucky day. Not wanting to lose the moment, Joe embraced her and made passionate love to her, right there against the kitchen countertop.

Afterward she said, "Thanks" and returned to the stove still wearing her tee shirt all pushed up around her neck.

Puzzled, Joe asked, "What was that all about?"

She explained, "The egg timer's broken."

* Joe walked into the kitchen and his wife smacked him on top of his head with a rolling pin. Joe said, "Honey? What was that for?!"

She said, "Well I was doing the laundry and I pulled out a piece of paper in your pocket with the name 'Billy Sue' written on it!"

"Honey, that's the name of a horse I got to bet on at the track." Joe's wife shrugs and walks away.

Three days later, Joe walks into the kitchen again and his wife smacks him in the head with a rolling pin. "Honey, what was that for?"

Wife said, "Your horse just called."

* An American couple are in the desert riding a camel when suddenly, the camel stops, and gets down on all fours and refuses to get up.

The couple get off and the man pulls the reins hard as he can, but the camel still lies there so he tries as hard as he can and jumps up and down, trying to get the camel to move. Then he pulls more and more but the camel won't budge.

The woman is standing behind the camel and says, "Hold on, stop pulling, let me try this." Suddenly, the camel jumps up and runs off like a bat out of hell.

"What did you just do?" The man asks.

"Well, I just kicked him hard between his legs on that bag-like thing that hangs down," she says.

The man gets up and turns his back to the woman and touches his toes and says, "Go ahead and do it!"

"Do what?" She says.

"Kick me in the same place because I've got to catch that f*ckin' camel!"

* Compromising does not mean you are wrong, and your wife is right.

It only means your health, safety, and general wellbeing are much more important than your ego.

* A husband stumbles through the door of his house several hours late after playing golf all day. His wife greets him at the door with an ominous look.

"Where were you?"

The golfer throws his arms up in the air and gives his wife this explanation, "I'm so sorry Honey. I finished my round and was putting my clubs in the trunk when I noticed a young woman fumbling by her car trying to fix her own flat tire. I offered to help her, and I changed her tire. She thanked me again and again, and we kept talking then we went to a bar, and the next thing I know I'm in bed with her at her place."

The wife stared at him, then said, "Don't you give me that crap, you played 36 holes today, didn't you!"

* A four-year-old boy after watching "The King and I" said to his mom, "When I grow up I'm going to have 5 wives, one who will cook, one who will wash, one who will clean up, one who will sing to me, and one who will go with me outside."

Mom replied, "Johnny, you also might want one to put you to sleep?"

"No mom, I will sleep with you."

A tear formed around Mom's eyes. "God bless you, Johnny." Mom whispered, then said, "But who will sleep with our 5 wives?"

"Let them sleep with Daddy," Johnny said.

A tear formed in Dad's eye. "God bless you, my son."

* A guy was standing in a bar and a man sits down next to him. After a while, they get to talking and at about 10:00 pm the second man says,

"Oh well, I better get home. My wife doesn't like me to stay out during the late night."

The first guy replies, "I'll help you out of this. I do this all the time when I'm out too late. Just do what I say. Go home and sneak into the bedroom. Get down and put your head between her legs then perform cunnilingus for about 20 minutes and there will be no complaints in the morning."

The man's not sure of whether to do this or not, but nods his head agreeing and continues to drink for another hour before heading home to give it a try.

When he gets home, the house is pitch black. He sneaks upstairs into the bedroom, pulls back the covers and proceeds to perform cunnilingus for 20 minutes.

The bed is like a swamp. He decides to get up and wash his face.

As he walks into the bathroom, his wife is sitting on the toilet.

Seeing her, he screams, "What the hell are you doing in here?!"

"Quiet!", she says. "You'll wake my mother."

* A man took his 5-year-old son to the zoo. The small boy watched the elephants roam in high grasses. The knee-high grass gave one large male elephant an erection and the small boy pointed to it and asked, "What's that?"

The man replied, "That is the elephant's private part. That's his penis."

The little boy was confused and said, "When mom brought me here, she told me it was 'nothing'".

The man smiled and simply said, "Your mother's spoiled."

* Joe was shaving in the locker room of his tennis club after several sets, when the club tennis pro, Bubba, walked in to take a piss. Joe couldn't help but notice when Bubba took out his penis it was huge!

Bubba finished and was washing his hands, when the golfer asked, "Bubba, I'll bet the girls like that one-eyed python of yours?"

"Yeah, keeps me busy," replied Bubba.

"Bubba, what's your secret to getting a big penis?"

Bubba replied, "Well, every night before I go to get in bed with a woman, I whack it on the bedpost three times."

So, Joe decided to try it that very night. He came in late, and his wife was asleep. Right before Joe got into bed, he beat his penis on the bedpost three times and his wife woke up and said, "Bubba, is that you?"

* If you know you are wrong about something and you don't belabor the point, you are a very wise person. If you right about something and you don't belabor the point, you are married.

* A long-time bachelor finally got married. He was very much in love, but it had been some time since he had been out on the town with his buddies. He said, "Honey baby, I'll be right back."

"Where are you off to my beautiful man," asks his wife?

"I'm going to the club bar, pretty face, and have a beer."

His new bride says, "Oh, you'd like to have a beer? Is that what you want my gallant, brave, and handsome man?"

His wife opens the refrigerator and reveals many bottles of beer from Germany, Spain, the US, Japan, Holland, etc.

He was surprised, then thinking quickly said, "Yes, my sweet...but at the bar...well, you know...they have frosted glasses..."

In the middle of his sentence, his wife said, "You want a frosted glass, my big strong man?"

She reached into the freezer and pulled out a large frosty beer mug.

That surprised him. "Yes, Toodles, my sweetheart, my dear, but at the bar they have those hors-d'oeuvres that are really delicious... I won't be long. OK?"

"You want hors-d'oeuvres, my big tootsie roll?" She opened the oven and took out two trays of hors d'oeuvres: chicken wings, mushroom caps, etc.

"But my dearest buttercup lammie pie... At the bar... You know...there's man's stuff, swearing, dirty words and all that..."

"Oooh! Yooou want dirty words you red-faced sh*tty d*ckhead?! Drink your f*cking slimy piss in this c*cksucking frozen mug and eat your motherf*cking snacks, because you are married now, and you aren't f*cking going anywhere! Got it Asswipe?"

* Joe's wife called out to him, "Sweetheart, I have to confess when I'm having sex with you, I think about other men."

Joe hears her as he sat reading a book, and without lifting his eyes, said, "Oh, you don't think of me? Well, when I have sex with other women, I'm thinking about you."

* Joe comes home and walks through the door and finds his wife waiting for him tapping her foot with an ominous look on her face.

"What's wrong honey?" He says as he closes the front door.

She is angry. She explains she found a pair of panties in her dresser that she's never seen before. She questions him relentlessly.

"Heck, I don't know. I was on a trip. I'm not the one who does the laundry! Honey, why don't you ask the housekeeper?"

The housekeeper comes in to clean the next day and the wife confronts her with the panties, angrily dangling them in the housekeeper's face.

"I don't have any idea where those panties came from!" The housekeeper shouts back at the wife.

The wife doesn't stop asking questions, "Well you're the only one here who does laundry, how did these get in my drawer?"

"Madam, those aren't my panties. I don't wear them - just ask your husband…."

* Joe's wife, Josephine, was sent to Paris to go to a one-week seminar for her job.

Joe drove her to the airport. "Have a great trip Jo!"

"Thank you, Joe, would you like me to get something for you in Paris?"

How about one of those young French babes!"

Jo had heard Joe before and still wasn't over his recent affair with the maid. She didn't say a word and went into the terminal.

One week later, Joe picked her up at the airport and asked, "So, Jo, how was the trip?"

"Very good, thank you."

"And, where's the present I asked you to bring back for me?"

"Present?"

"Haha! You know that French babe I wanted?" Joe said.

"Oh, that? Well, I remembered that and Joe, you're going to have to wait 9 months to see if it's a girl."

* If you and your wife need a change of pace, or want to do something totally different, try the sport of "Wife Carrying" or "Eukonkanto" which began in Finland in the late 19th Century.

Wife carrying originated from ancient gangs of Finnish robbers who would steal food and women from different villages and keep the women as their wives.

The sport of wife carrying has now spread worldwide. The US Championships takes place in the second weekend of July in Menahga, Minnesota and the World Championship of wife carrying takes place in Finland.

The winning couple is the one who completes the 250 meters course the fastest. The course must have two difficult obstacles to climb over and one water carry-through, with a depth of at least a meter. The husband must carry his wife all through the course. Fastest time is the winner.

The wife must weigh at least 49 kgs. The winner wins beer equal to the weight of the wife.

* Joe picked up the phone and listened for two seconds then said, "Well, I don't know. Check the weather yourself!" Then Joe slammed the phone down.

"Who was it?' asks Josephine.

"Wrong number. It was some asshole wanting to know if the coast was clear."

* "I met my wife at a singles bar," Joe said.

"Really? I met my wife that way too."

"I don't think so," said Joe, "When I met my wife at the bar, she was supposed to be home with the kids."

Masturbation

* "When it comes to sex: some men treat women as objects; some women treat objects as men."

- Mokokoma Mokhonoana

* Masturbation? I can't do that anymore since I threw my back out masturbating.

- Chelsea Handler

* "Sir," said a very nervous young man, "I would like to ask for your daughter's hand."

"What the f*ck? I don't understand you boy. Yu sayin' you don't got no f*ckin' hand?"

"No, sir. I've got a hand but I'm tired of using it."

Mathematics

*A renowned Mathematics Professor planned to fly away for a vacation during a break between semesters.

When he passed the airport security, it was discovered he was carrying a bomb in his carry-on luggage and was arrested.

"Professor, we don't understand this. You have had a very successful career, a family man, a credit to society. Why on earth would you try to carry a bomb on the plane?"

"Very sorry," the professor said. "I was not trying to blow up the plane."

"Yeah, right. So why the bomb?"

"I'll explain," the professor said. Proven statistics show the probability of a bomb being on an airplane is 1/100,000. Also, statistics show there 500,000 passengers on flights at any given time. Therefore, there is a relatively high probability of a bomb being on a plane. And, that probability is so high that I don't have any peace of mind on a flight." Said the professor.

"Well, I doubt that but even if it were true, what does it have to do with you trying to bring a bomb in your carry-on?"

"If the probability of one bomb on a plane is 1/100,000, and I bring another bomb on the plane, the chance of two bombs is 1/10,000,000, and I am much safer."

* Three professors are discussing whether it's better to have a wife or a mistress.

The French professor insists it's better to have a mistress: "It's more exciting, your life is always passionate, full of romance!"

The Philosophy professor disagreed, "No, it is far better to have a wife. Your love grows deep, you live with your best friend, there are few unpleasant surprises."

The Math professor listened to them for a while, then said, "Actually, if you ask me, it's best to have both."

The other two professors are surprised. "Why is that?" asked the French professor.

"It is self-evident." Said the math professor. "You have more freedom since your mistress will think you are with your wife and vice-versa."

* "Hey, you sh*thead! Stay away from my girlfriend. Do you want problems?

"Yeah! Yeah, I want problems!"

"Okay! For all real numbers b and c such that the product of c and 3 is b, how do you express the sum of c and 3 in terms of b?"

Men

* Joe just got into a relationship with a married woman, and her husband was away so they met at her house, and they made love for hours. Then the phone rang.

"Hello?" She said. "Oh, hi... You are where? Oh, that's nice and I'm glad you're having a great time. Love you too. Take care, Bye."

She hangs up the telephone and Joe asked her, "Who was it?"

"Oh, that was my husband telling me all about the great hunting trip he's on with you."

* What is the similarity between a clitoris, a wedding anniversary, and a toilet bowl - Men usually miss all of them.

* My wife is extremely jealous and keeps thinking I'm having an affair with my ex-girlfriend.

I tell her not to be concerned with those thoughts.

By the way, I do see my ex-girlfriend now and then, but I don't ever cheat on both my wife and ex-girlfriend."

Mental Health Facility

* I was walking with a friend past a mental hospital when I heard lots of people inside yelling "87! 87! 87!" You couldn't see them because of the 12-foot solid security fence surrounding the facility.

My friend noticed a hole in the fence and decided he wanted to see what the commotion was about. As he peered through the hole, he saw an ass - someone was mooning him.

He reeled back startled and shocked. Then the chant changed to "88! 88! 88!"

Neighbors

* A man appeared before a judge after his arrest and was being charged with several crimes.

"You are charged with murdering your mother-in-law with a chainsaw."

From the back of the courtroom, a man shouts out, "You stinkin' lying asshole!"

"Order in the court!" The judge said. Then the judge said, "You are also charged with bashing the door to door salesman with a shovel."

Again, from the back of the courtroom, a man shouts, "You no good stinking bastard!"

"Order in the court!" The judge snapped. Then the judge continued, "You are also charged with killing your wife with an electric drill."

Again, the judge hears, "You are a deceitful prick!"

The judge stops the arraignment proceeding and says, "You in the back, stand up. I'm going to hold you in contempt. Why are your shouting in my courtroom?"

"I've lived next door to that dishonest, mendacious, perfidious, deceitful, deceiving, two-faced jerkoff for 5 years but do you think he ever had any of those tools when I just wanted to borrow one of them for an hour?"

New Yorkers

* A New Yorker and a Texan, both high handicap golfers, were spraying their shots into the rough. The Texan was driving the golf cart and drove through the rough terrain and both players were bouncing around.

It got so bumpy the New Yorker kept hitting his head on the cart's roof and eventually fell out of the cart.

"Hey, take it easy man. This ain't a rodeo," the New Yorker said as he got up rubbing the top of his head.

"Sh*t, pardner, you ought to learn bronc riding," said the Texan.

The New Yorker said, "Sounds great but there are no rodeos in the Big Apple."

"You don't need a rodeo. Just get your girlfriend down on her hands and knees, then ride up on her, if you know what I mean. Then reach round and cup both of her breasts and whisper, 'Your sister has bigger ones', then try to hold on for eight seconds!"

News Media

* In Russia, there are only two TV channels. Channel One contains nothing but government propaganda.

On Channel Two, a uniformed KGB agent comes up on the screen and says, "Go back to Channel One!"

* Freedom of speech in Russia is just like oral sex. You surpass it a little and you're in the arse.

* I wonder why newscasters don't ever curse. It's almost impossible. There are pauses in speaking where sometimes you just must put in a four-letter word.

For example, if I were giving the news, I'd say, "Those motherf*ckers flew the f*ckin plane into the World Trade Center. We should kill those motherf*cking assholes."

But newscasters don't say that, and I wonder how they hold themselves back if they are human? I mean, I suspect they are robots or zombies.

- Nick Hornby

No Respect

* "When my mother would put me in the sandbox to play, the cat kept trying to cover me up."

- Rodney Dangerfield

Payback

* I got hit with an octopus in Detroit one time when we played the Detroit Red Wings. It was very gross. I hadn't had anything that gross ever happen to me. I got it right in the back of the neck and all the juice was coming down. It was awful. How the hell did they come up with an octopus?

- Pat Burns, NHL Coach

* Sometimes it's best to move on when relationships go south, immature Joe thought

otherwise. Joe had a high school sweetheart, but they separated after graduation. Joe went to a college on the West Coast, and she went to a college on the East Coast.

They tried to stay in touch and be faithful to each other and see each other when they could. But as time went on, the emails grew less and less. Joe would email her but wouldn't get an email back for days.

She had met another and finally emailed Joe she would like to date others and wished him well. Joe was heartbroken, and she wouldn't respond but he continued to email her, then wound up trying to visit her at college unannounced but she avoided him. Joe continued to email her, and she became annoyed and got sick of him pestering her.

She decided to get rid of him once and for all, so she did a selfie picture of herself giving a guy a blowjob and emailed it to Joe with a note, "Joe, I've got a new boyfriend now so please leave me alone."

Joe was outraged so he forwarded just the photo to her parents using her email address with a note, "Dear Mom and Dad, having a great time at college, please send more money!"

Octopus

* An octopus walked into a Scottish nightclub where a band was playing. The octopus sat down at the bar and listened to the band.

The Scottish band took a break and the octopus walked over to the band and said, "I'm the greatest musician in the world. I can play any musical instrument better than you."

The Scottish bandleader handed the octopus a guitar and he played it better than anyone ever had before using all his limbs and made the guitar sound amazing. Then handed back the guitar.

The band leader got up from his piano and said, "Oh, well let's see how you do on the keyboard."

The octopus sat down and played the piano as if 2 pianos were playing at the same time as no one had ever heard before.

Finally, the leader said, "Okay, okay, let's see how you do on this!" Then he handed the octopod a set of bagpipes.

The octopod struggled with it and couldn't seem to hold it properly turning every which way. After several minutes, the octopus still fumbled.

"Looks like you're not the greatest musician in the world – you can't play the bagpipes!"

The octopus was out of breath and said, "Play this? I'm gonna f*ck her when I get her pajamas off."

Optimism

* Oh, I don't know if I'm an optimist or a pessimist. When I look at the glass, it's only half clean and half dirty.

* I may be going to hell, but at least the dinners won't ever be served cold.

* Yes, I know my illness is terminal. I will be dying soon. I look at like finally, I'm getting closer to becoming a zombie.

Penguins

* A truck driver is driving a few penguins to a zoo. Before he gets into town his truck breaks down. Frantically he waves down a passing motorist.

"Thanks for stopping man! You gotta help me out. I was taking these penguins to the zoo, but my truck broke down. These penguins need to get to the zoo. Will you take them there? I'll catch up with you as soon as it's fixed. Here's some money, here. Will you do this for me?"

The man agrees. The penguins waddle into the back seat, and off they go.

Eventually, the truck driver gets his truck fixed and goes to the zoo to catch up. But none of the penguins are there, and neither is the motorist who helped him out.

The truck driver jumps back in his truck and drives around town, searching for the penguins. Finally, he sees the motorist strolling down a sidewalk with all the penguins behind him. The truck driver pulls over and starts yelling, "What are you doing, man? These penguins are supposed to be in the zoo!"

"I did!" said the motorist. "Then I had some money left over, and I thought they'd like to see a movie."

Pessimists

* An optimist usually thinks we are in the best of all possible worlds. Ironically, the pessimist also believes this but fears this is true.

- James Branch Cabell

* What's worse than finding a bug in your apple? A. Finding a huge green slimy worm in your apple.

So, what's worse than that? A. Finding half of a huge green slimy worm in your apple?

* While those assholes were arguing over whether the glass of beer was half-empty or half-full, I drank the beer. Call me an opportunist.

Pilots

* Passengers on a small plane were getting impatient waiting for the pilots to board the plane. They finally came on the plane using the middle door and slowly walked up to the cockpit.

The passengers were taken aback because both pilots looked like they were sight impaired. One pilot was wearing dark glasses and had a guide dog and was brushing into passengers as he walked to the cockpit. The other pilot was also wearing dark glasses and his arms were outstretched as he felt his way up the aisle.

The passengers couldn't believe what was going on. Was this a joke? The passengers looked at each other nervously and started mumbling and asked the flight attendants if this was for real.

Suddenly, the plane's engines roared as they accelerated down the runway. People started to yell, some passengers were crying, and some were praying.

As the plane was reaching the end of the runway, people were yelling louder and getting hysterical. When they almost reached the end of the runway, everyone let out a hair-raising and roaring scream!

Then the plane lifted off!

In the cockpit, the copilot said to the captain. "One of these days, these buggers aren't going to let out a roaring scream and we'll have no idea when to take off."

Play on Words

* All generalizations are bad.

-R.H. Grenier

* A string walks into a bar and sits and says "bartender, give me a scotch on the rocks!"

The bartender stares at him and says, looks at him and says, "What the hell? You are a string!

The string says, "Yes, I am a string."

"Well, you have to leave."

The next day...the string wants to have a beer and goes back to the bar, sits down, and says to the bartender, "Give me a scotch on the rocks!"

The bartender looks at him and says "I thought I told you yesterday, we don't serve your kind here. If I see you here again I'm calling the cops!"

The string leaves, but still wants a beer. So, the string decides to wear a disguise. He ties himself up in a bunch of knots like a monkey's fist, but one last piece of string is sticking out and fuzzy.

The string goes back into the bar, sits down, and says, "Bartender, give me a scotch on the rocks!"

The bartender stares at him and says, "Aren't you that string I've been kicking out of here?" that's been hanging around here lately?"

The string looks him straight in the eye and says, "No, I'm a frayed knot."

* A monster walked into a bar, sat down, and yelled, "Hey bartender, Give me a beer right now!"

The bartender said, "Sorry, we don't allow people like you – you are a monster."

"I said, give me a beer," the monster roared!

"No. I can clearly see you are a monster and I'm not serving you." The bartender replied.

Still persisting, the monster looked at a woman at the end of the bar. "Bartender, you see that lady at the end of the bar? Well, I'm going to eat her and then I'm going to eat you if you don't give me a beer right now!"

"Go ahead!" Said the bartender.

The monster rushed the woman and chewed her up and swallowed her.

The monster looked over to the bartender. "How come you're not afraid of me?" He asked as he tried to approach the bartender. The monster was getting slower and slower almost falling asleep.

"Because that was a bar-bitch-you-ate." Said the bartender.

* A mushroom walked into a dance club and asked a girl to dance.

The girl refused and said, "Are you joking? You are a mushroom!"

"Oh, come on. I am a fun guy!"

* He could cell RNA to a ribosome.

* Joe was in a bad car accident and almost died. He recovered at the hospital, but he lost an eye, so they gave him a wooden eye until a glass eye could be made up.

Joe was depressed and didn't do much. His friends came around and persuaded him to go out to a bar to have some fun.

At the bar, Joe sat there staring at his beer. One of his friends said, "Hey look at that cute girl over there. Joe, go and ask her to dance."

"Nope, not me," Joe said. She wouldn't dance with me – a guy with a wooden eye."

"What about the girl over there?" His friend said.

"Oh no. She's got a huge nose. Looks like she's eating a banana!" Joe sat there, then despite the big nose, he got up and walked over to her.

"Do you want to dance?" Joe asked.

The girl got very excited at being asked to dance by Joe, who was a very good-looking man and shouted, "Would I! Would I!"

Joe took offense and walked away saying, "Big nose! Big nose!"

* Joe walked into a bar and the bartender said, "What would you like to drink?"

Joe said, "Whiskey." The bartender poured him a whiskey and Joe downed it.

"That will be $8.00," said the bartender.

"What?!" Joe said. "You asked me what I would like to drink? Why I thought you were buying me a drink?"

"Get out of my bar," said the bartender and Joe left.

A year later, Joe walked into the same bar. The bartender looked at him and said, "You're the jackoff who came in here last year and conned me out of a drink. Get the hell out."

"Why I've haven't ever been in this place in my life," Joe said.

"Oh, ah, sorry, it's my mistake. What would you like?"

"Well, Thank you. Give me a whiskey."

Politics

* Joe got divorced and married Jane. This was Joe's second marriage and Jane's third.

On their wedding night, Jane said, "Joe, please be gentle."

"What?" Joe replied.

Jane looked at him shyly and said, "It's my first time."

Joe laughed, "You, a virgin? You've been married three times?"

Jane explained. "My first husband was a philosopher and he only talked about it."

"But your second husband was a doctor?"

"That's right," said Jane. "He was a gynecologist – he only looked at it. And my third husband was an engineer, and he took over a year to design a new way to do it."

"Why didn't you ever ask me about sex?" Joe asked.

"Well, I married you since I knew you were going to f*ck me just like you do to your constituents every day."

*Thirty politicians are traveling to a meeting by a train going through a rural farm area which derails and crashes.

A farmer who witnesses it all from his field decides to bury them all.

A few hours later, news media and the authorities swarm the farm. The police ask the farmer what happened to the thirty politicians.

"I buried them all," he replies.

"Were they all dead then?" The police ask.

"Well, some of them said they weren't, but you know how they always lie!"

* Bill Clinton was campaigning for Hillary near an upper midwestern wintery, snowy city.

After a rousing speech, Bill returned to his suite. Standing and posing proudly looking out of the suite to ground below, he noticed that written in 'yellow' in the snow drift outside was, "Bill Clinton is an ass."

Exploding into a rage, Bill called his Secret Service people to immediately get a sample of the 'yellow snow' and find out whose urine it was. The Secret Service jumped into action taking samples and pictures.

The Secret Service returned shortly. Trump jumped up angrily and demanded an immediate report.

The Secret Service agent, a little reluctant said, "Bill, we know whose urine was used in the message."

"Who was it!" demanded Bill.

The agent responded, "The urine is Donald Trump's." Bill flew into another rage.

The agent, now even more reluctant to speak said, "Bill there's more information."

"What the hell could be worse?" Bill shouted.

The agent replied, "The handwriting was Hillary's!"

* Obama invited Trump to play golf with two of Obama's regular golf friends.

One of his friends asked him, "Does Trump really has a 5 handicap?"

"He's very good," Obama replied.

Trump is waiting for them at the first tee and after introductions to the two friends of Obama, Trump began and sliced his first tee shot into deep foliage and the ball went right into the middle of thick bushes.

One friend of Obama's whispered, "You said he was a good golfer!"

Obama said, "Just watch him play."

Trump stood near the thick clump of bushes determining the distance to the green. He grabbed a club from his bag and walked through the deep rough and then went directly into the deep foliage carrying an iron.

They watched in amazement as his body separated the heavy foliage. They saw an iron raise out of the top of the bushes, then heard the swish of a mighty swing. Then the sound of the cracking of small branches, the tearing of leaves, and a sharp click as the ball is struck.

One of them pointed to the green and there was his ball rolling on to the front of the green and stopped within two feet of the pin. Trump made an easy birdie.

On the second hole, a par-3, The Donald hit the ball into the middle of the lake.

The two friends looked at Obama again and say, "A five handicap? Really? You said he was good."

Obama replied, "Just watch, he's a great player."

Donald walked right into the lake after his ball. One minute passed and there was no sign of him. Suddenly they see a stretched-out hand come out of the water. One of Obama's friends shouted out, "You better dive into the lake to save him because he's drowning!"

Obama replied, "No... that just means he wants a 5-iron."

* The Queen invited Donald Trump to visit her in Buckingham Palace. As he descended the stairs off Air Force One, the Queen greeted him after she was driven up in a Royal horse-drawn carriage.

"Welcome to Britain, President Trump."

"Well, thank you, your Majesty, for the invitation."

With both seated in the carriage, they're off toward the Palace. While they were talking, one of the horses let go a flatulent blast and they continued to casually talk through the filthy smell. Neither of them said anything.

After the air cleared, the Queen remarked, "Even in a Royal procession, sometimes things go wrong. I'm sure you understand."

Trump says, "Not a problem, your majesty, it wasn't until you said something, I thought the horse did it."

Porn

* A film director's new film was banned by the censorship board in a large city. He asked for a meeting and explained his film which was being privately shown to the board wasn't a bit pornographic.

A board member stopped the film on a single frame at the very beginning of it and said, "Do you mean to tell this picture is not pornographic?"

The director said, "Why haven't you ever seen 9 people in love before?"

Poverty

* When I was a young man in the entertainment world, I was so poor I went to orgies just to eat the grapes.

- Rodney Dangerfield

* When I was a kid, I was so poor we used to visit my rich grandma in the poor house for the homeless.

* We were so poor, every Christmas we got a piece of paper with the word "coal" written on it.

* We were so poor we would open our junk mail to eat spam.

* We were so poor when we went to KFC we licked other people's fingers.

Practical

* Joe looked out into his backyard one day and was astonished to see a gorilla in his tree. He

didn't know what the hell to do, so on a whim, he googled "Gorilla Removers," and was surprised to see a listing nearby his house.

He called Gorilla Removers. "I have a gorilla in the tree in my backyard." Joe said.

The man asked, "Can you tell if it's male or female?" The man asked.

Joe looked at the gorilla then said, "Male, I think."

"OK, I can help. Be right over."

A short time later, a truck pulled up and a man got out carrying a ladder, a pole, and a shotgun and leading a dog.

"OK," the man said, "Here's how it works. I climb up in the tree and push the gorilla out with this pole. When he hits the ground, this dog is specially trained to grab the gorilla by the gonads and render him helpless. But I need you to hold this loaded shotgun."

"Why?" Joe asked.

"You'll see." The gorilla remover climbed the tree and poked the gorilla with the pole. The gorilla simply turned and pushed the man out of the tree.

As he was falling, he yelled out at Joe, "Quick! Shoot the dog! Shoot the dog!"

Prescriptions

* Prescriptions require full disclosure on possible side effects which make taking drugs a bit dangerous. For example, Joe couldn't sleep so he went to the doctor for a prescription for sleeping pills.

When he read the label, the possible side effects were amnesia and paranoia.

Now, when Joe's wife asks him how he slept, he replies, "I don't remember how I slept and who sent you?"

* Joe had a terrible headache which he couldn't get rid of, so he went to the doctor who prescribed a drug to treat headaches.

When Joe read the pamphlet, which came with the drug and the first side effect was that the drug may cause headaches.

Joe didn't understand that. He went to the doctor to get a remedy for his headache and was given a drug that may cause headaches.

Joe went back to his doctor and said, "What the hell! I still have a headache and you prescribed a drug that causes headaches! That's like me going to the hospital emergency room with a stab wound and you giving me a few more thrusts with the scalpel!"

Priests and Preachers

* The preacher asked his congregation for someone to testify if their prayers were answered and a young woman raised her hand.

"Mrs. Jones, please tell us about it," the preacher asked.

"Several weeks ago, my husband fell off a ladder and crushed his scrotum. He was in terrible pain. Our doctor did the best he could but had to refer him to two more doctors. He was in so much pain, we had to help him around the house. He couldn't work and anytime he moved, he suffered so much pain."

She continued her story even though the men in church started to shift uncomfortably listening to her.

"I prayed and prayed as my husband had to go through several operations. The doctors were able to put together the pieces of his scrotum and keep things in place with a strong metal wire."

A few groans were heard from the men in the congregation.

"Thanks to the prayers of our family, he is almost recovered but still has to take it very easy. But his scrotum should heal."

Her husband was sitting next to her and stood up and said, "Hi everyone, I'm her husband and I just want to say the correct word for my wife's story is sternum."

* A Bishop, a Minister and a Rabbi went hiking on a very hot and humid day.

It was so hot, they thought they were the only ones around. Perspiring profusely, they came up to a clear small river running through the middle of the fairway.

The bishop said, "I've got to cool off." So, he took his clothes off and jumped into the water. "Ah, that's refreshing!" the bishop said as he cooled off in the water.

The Minister and the Rabbi likewise took their clothes off and jumped in as well.

They all felt better, but as they were climbing out of the river, a group of ladies came through the woods also hiking.

They scrambled for their clothes but were only able to grab their shirts as the ladies passed by. The bishop and minister covered their genitals. The Rabbi draped his shirt over his face.

The Bishop and the Minister sheepishly grinned at the ladies as they passed them. The bishop asked the Rabbi, "Why did you cover your face rather than your genitals?"

The Rabbi said, "I'm not sure about you two guys, but in my temple, they know my face."

Private Parts

* Charlie was a wealthy bachelor who loved to play golf. Lots of girls were after him but he was extremely shy since he had a very small penis.

While playing at his exclusive Country Club, Charlie got a hole in one on the 5th hole. He was ecstatic over his first hole in one, yet disappointed no one saw it. He glumly walked up to the green to get his ball out of the hole when a genie popped out.

"This is one of the most exclusive courses in the world and has everything, including the services of a genie if you make a hole in one by yourself and no one sees it. Because you've just made one I will grant you one wish for anything your heart desires."

Charlie was overjoyed! He thought for a bit, then said, "I want a longer penis."

"Your wish is granted," said the genie.

As Charlie continued his round, he could feel his penis grow longer. By the time he finished the 18th hole, his penis came out beneath his shorts and reached down below his knees.

"Whoa!" Charlie thought, "Maybe this wasn't such a great wish after all?"

Charlie wanted to see the genie, so he grabbed a golf cart and loaded it up with buckets of balls and drove back to the 5th hole and began to hit balls at the pin.

It was almost dark when finally, he hit a hole in one. By the time he got to the green, his penis was dragging on the ground.

Sure enough, the genie appeared as he took his ball out of the cup.

The genie began to give the same speech, "This is one of the most exclusive courses in the world and has everything, including the services of a genie if you make a hole in one all alone, and because you've just made one I will grant you…"

The genie recognized Charlie and said, "Oh, it's you again. You must really want something. What's going on?"

"Could you make my legs longer?" said Charlie.

Problems

* If a problem can be solved then there's no use worrying about it, but if a problem can't be solved then what's the use of worrying.

* Having problems is like putting yourself in a washing machine. It throws you around back and forth and turns you all around and winds up spinning you at high speeds. And, when you're done you come out cleaner, better and brighter than before. And wiser as well.

Procrastination

* "If procrastination was a sport, I would compete in it later." - Anon.

* A thought just occurred to me. If I had spent the time doing the things I am procrastinating about them (instead of spending that time just procrastinating about it), I would have accomplished a hell of a lot more in my life.

Wow, that thought is profound. I'm going to lay down and think about that thought.

* A recent study by Professor Adam Grant, shows that even though most everyone feels procrastination is bad (and in many ways it is), he believes people who put things off until the last minute are more creative than those who do things on schedule.

In other words, people who do things when they have time to do them are less creative in doing the task. Studies have shown who had less time to do the task, were generally more creative than those who had more time to do them.

He believes that when people feel pressure, they usually go with their first thought (which usually is on target). Those who have time to mull over their first thought tend to get away from the most direct answer or solution on ways to do the tasks.

Studies have shown those who put things off until the last minute get the task done much faster than they would if they had more time to do the task.

Professor Frank Partnoy wrote a book, "The Art and Science of Delay," where he explains procrastination (or as he refers to it as "managing delay") by people who manage delay gather more information on how the task should be done and last-minute brainstorming usually works better to come up with the best solution to doing the task.

However, there are negative effects of procrastination and working under stress. Stress in general is unhealthy. Constant procrastinators have been found to be overall less healthy than those who don't procrastinate a lot. There are other studies which show students who procrastinate generally get lower grades as well.

Reincarnation

* A young boy told an old man, "Yeah, well, I didn't believe in reincarnation when I was your age, either."

* Three men died and went to the pearly gates. Before they were let in, St Peter gave them all a chance to return to earth reincarnated as an animal or a plant or a tree or anything organic. If they

wanted to be an animal, they could pick any animal they wanted. They had to jump off the clouds and callout the name of the animal they wished to become.

The first man chose a lion and jumped off a cloud and called out "Lion," and instantly found himself in an African Jungle as King of the Beasts.

The second man chose to be an elephant and jumped off a cloud and called out, "Elephant," and instantly found himself deep in an Indian Jungle. He could fully remember his prior life and he was even wiser now as an elephant than he was when he was human.

The third man slipped off a cloud and said, "Sh*t!"

* You can always tell if a deceased person believed in reincarnation by looking at their tombstone. Instead "Rest in Peace" or "RIP", you will see "BRB" or "Be Right Back."

* "Yes, well, there was a time when I believed in reincarnation, but that was many, many years ago – a very long time ago - in some other life."

- Dave Schinbeckler

* Men work very hard to attain money go to extremes and that at times will create health problems. As they grow older they sacrifice their hard-earned money to try to regain their health.

Is that really living? Men who work hard for a living constantly worry about the future and at times so much so, they forget about being in the present. This results in men not really being in the present or the future. It is as if a hard-working dedicated man will become so obsessed with his goal, he will forget about the present or the future and tragically die never having really lived.

Reincarnation relates to interdependence rebirth and the laws of cause and effect.

- The Dalai Lama

Religion

* There were four churches in a small town, an Evangelical Church, a Baptist Church, a Church

of the Latter-Day Saints, and a Catholic Church and all four churches were overrun with mice.

The Evangelical Church called a meeting to decide how to get rid of the mice. After much discussion and prayer, they decided the mice were put there by God and decided to do nothing so as not to interfere with God's will.

The Baptist Church officials decided to put the mice in the baptistery and drown them, but the mice sneaked out and afterward there were three times the number of holy mice running around the Church

The Church of the Latter-Day Saints decided they did not want to hurt God's creations, so they captured all the mice and drove them miles away and released them. Several days later, the mice came back and brought back more mice with them.

The Priests in the Catholic Church discussed and prayed what to do with the huge number of mice and after much prayer and deliberation, they decided to baptize all the mice as Catholics and make them parishioners of the Church. The mice now only visit the Church on Easter and Christmas.

* If you tell the world there is an invisible man who created everything and one day when they die they will go to heaven, most of the people on earth will believe you. Ironically, these are the same people who pass a wet paint sign and must touch the wall to see if the paint is dry.

- George Carlin

* It has been said Religion is like a man's sex organ – a penis. It's great to have one and great to be proud of it. But you don't go waving it around in public or try to force it on someone.

- Anon.

Research

* I haven't failed. I've just found 10,000 ways that aren't going to do the job.

- Thomas A. Edison

* A jealous woman does more extensive and thorough research than the local police, the FBI, the CIA, the NSA, the KGB, Mi6, Nielsen, and perhaps God Himself.

- Anon.

* Officer, I am not in any way stalking him. I am merely doing social research.

Riddles

* Q. What do prophylactics and caskets have in common?

A. They are both filled with stiff meat only one is coming and the other is going.

* Q: What are the most common said last words of a redneck?

A: Hold my beer and watch this!

* Q. What is it that you can hold but can't ever touch?

A. Your breath.

* Q. What is it that only exists in light yet disappears when you shine light on it?

A. A Shadow

* Someone told me once the ability to solve riddles shows a sane and logical mind. I enjoy riddles and take them seriously.

- Stephen King, The Waste Lands

Romantic

* No, I'm not offended if you say I have a small penis. That's just the way I am and really can't do much about it. By the way, I'll bet my penis even

looks tinier compared to some of the sh*ts you've taken. – Anon.

* Men complain on how complicated women are. My girlfriend is very simple to understand. She only wants two things. The first is faithfulness to her. Unwavering loyalty. And I have a look for any woman who tries to flirt with me that instantly makes the flirting stop.

The second thing my girlfriend wants is orgasms. Those are the only two things she wants. Oh, wait, money. I've got to remember money.

* It's been said the story of "Fifty Shades of Gray" is only romantic because the man is fabulously wealthy. If you take the same story but the man is a penniless redneck, it's strictly a porn BDSM tale. Money must be very romantic.

* A customer asked an attractive single lady cashier if there was any change in interest depending on when he first makes a deposit compared to when he withdraws.

The attractive lady cashier said, "Sir, interest doesn't depend on when you put in or when you take it out, it depends on how long it has been in."

* Most all of us have some weirdness and when we meet another whose weirdness is compatible with ours, it's called love.

- Dr. Seuss

Salespersons

* A barber will always prepare and lather up a man well (with sincere approbation and praise) before he shaves him.

- Dale Carnegie

*People who sell:

* He could sell a parachute to Superman.

* He could sell a glass a water to a drowning man.

* He could sell an Oculus Rift virtual reality headset to Stevie Wonder.

* He could sell a hairbrush to Vin Diesel, Yul Brenner, Gandhi, Michael Jordan, and Mike Tyson and have them all fight over who is going to buy the first one.

* He could sell a ketchup Popsicle to a lady wearing white gloves and a white wedding dress on her way to the altar a hot day in July.

People who can't sell:

* You couldn't sell a vagina to Bruce Jenner.

* You couldn't sell a hamster in a bathhouse.

* Partially quoting Abraham Lincoln, the Sales Manager announced, "'You can fool all the people some of the time...'" The manager continued, "Oh, by the way, those are the exact people we want to concentrate on."

* Seriously, salesmanship is boundless and keeps the world turning for everyone. Our day to day living is selling. We are all salespeople.

- James Cash Penney

Santa Claus

* Christmas Progressions in life:

You begin by believing in Santa Claus.

As you grow older, you no longer believe in Santa Claus.

Then you dress like Santa Claus in a red suit and a white beard.

Finally, you look like Santa Claus.

* If you are a true man, you can do all your Christmas shopping 20 minutes before the stores close on Christmas Eve for all your 15 relatives.

School Fun

* "When I was a kid in the 4th grade, I was asked to name all the presidents? Hey, all of the presidents already had a name!"

- Demitri Martin

* A grade schoolteacher was giving her class a lesson on enjoying and using your senses to make them remember to smell the roses as they go through life.

She gave the class several different flavors of small pieces of hard candy and told them to close their eyes before putting each piece of candy in their mouth. "After you taste the candy, tell me what flavor it is."

Class members easily identified the common flavors like lime, chocolate, cherry, lemon and so on. But when she gave them all a honey flavored candy, no one knew what the flavor was.

She decided to give them a hint. "The name of the flavor is the same name that your mom calls your dad a lot."

A little boy in the back yelled out, "Spit it out! They're assholes!"

* High school teachers are very strict. They tell you again and again, "Don't drink alcohol", don't do any drugs, and don't be promiscuous and sleep with everyone."

High school teachers tell you these things, so you can get good grades, graduate, and go to college where you can do all these.

* On Friday afternoon, the teacher was having trouble getting the attention of her class. Her students were not paying any attention to her and watched the clock as it neared 3pm. Frustrated, she said, "Whoever answers the next question can go home early."

Little Joey got up and threw a book out the window.

"Who threw that?" the Teacher demanded.

"I did," said little Joey and promptly walked out the door.

* Little Joey was caught by the teacher when he was making ugly faces at the girls.

"Joey, did you know when you make ugly faces, your face could freeze like that for the rest of your life?" The teacher said.

Joey replied, "Oh, I see no one warned you."

Self-Help

* I was determined all my life to keep improving at whatever I chose to do. I thought and thought on ways to keep improving and I decided to dedicate my life to ways of self-help.

My first step in my quest for self-improvement was to visit the largest bookstore in my area having thousands and thousands of books on every subject you could think of. When I walked into the huge store, I was amazed at how large the store was. Wandering around the store, I stopped a salesperson named "Joe" and asked him where in this massive store, I could find self-help books. Did they have a special section dedicated solely to self-help books?

Joe replied, "I would like to help you, but if I did, that would defeat the purpose.

* One of the reasons I discuss things with myself is because I'm the only one whose answers I accept when I want an expert opinion."

- George Carlin

* If you want to self-help yourself, find love since when you are in love, your whole being is open to everything in life. If you want to find love, you must first love yourself, with all your imperfections. If you can't accept yourself, you will have difficulty in accepting others with their imperfections.

- John Lennon

* Then again, the first step in helping yourself, may be to accept yourself. We should certainly accept who we are as long as we aren't serial killers.

- Ellen DeGeneres

* Always, understand people look out for themselves - so you shouldn't ever ask a barber if you need a haircut.

- Warren Buffett

* Some people wonder about the true meaning of life. They want to help themselves understand the meaning of life. I think that's the wrong question to ask if you want to help yourself and it's a stupid question.

Life just exists. You might tell yourself; I'm trying to become better and cannot accept I mean nothing. Subconsciously, you know that is bullshit.

I see life the same as I see dancing. Dancing doesn't have any meaning. You are simply dancing because you enjoy it and its fun. Understanding that is helping yourself.

- Jackie Mason

Senior Fun

* The police broke up a prostitution ring at an exclusive Florida Resort on a late summer afternoon and lined up 10 girls they just arrested outside on the driveway entrance to the resort.

The grandmother of one of the girls was going by slowly walking with her cane when she noticed her granddaughter standing in line.

"Why are you standing in line, my dear?" Grandma asked.

Not wanting to tell her grandma what was going on, she replied, "Grandma, the police are giving away free oranges and we are standing in line for them."

"Why that's awfully nice of them. I'd like get some too, so I'll stand in line with you."

A policeman was going down the line asking each girl for identification and other details from all the prostitutes. When he got to Grandma he said,

"Wow, grandma! You still going at this at your age?"

Grandma smiled and said, "Oh, it's easy. I just take out my teeth and suck them dry."

* Joe decided to become a minister and loved to give sermons to his Sunday congregation. He talked one Sunday about forgiveness and preached on and on. He asked the congregation to raise their hands to find out how many in the congregation were willing to forgive their enemies.

Only a few of the congregation raised their hands. So, Joe went on longer preaching it is best in the eyes of God to forgive your enemies. After 20 minutes more of his preaching, he asked again for a show of hands. This time he got a show of 75% of the congregation.

So, Joe continued to preach on forgiveness for another 20 minutes, then finally asked for a show of hands on how many were willing to forgive their enemies.

Everyone raised their hands except one little old woman seated in the back of the church.

Joe looked at her and said, "Why don't you want to forgive your enemies?"

"I don't have a single enemy," she said.

"Wow!" Joe said. "That's fantastic and may I ask your age?"

"I'm 99," Mrs. Smith replied.

"That's fantastic! In your 99 years, you don't have any enemies! Mrs. Smith, would you come up here and tell the congregation how you managed in your 99 years to not to have an enemy on this good earth?"

Mrs. Smith slowly went up the aisle to the front and then turned around to everyone and said, "I just outlived the f*ckin' bitches."

* Q: What can a man do during the very difficult times when his wife is having annoying hot flashes and experiencing menopause?

A. Keep busy. If you're handy with tools, you can finish the basement. When you're done, make sure you build it very comfortable as you will need a place to live.

* An elderly woman followed a young man through a supermarket who was carrying a small basket to buy a few things.

The young guy couldn't help but notice he was being followed by her. So, as he got in the checkout line he noticed the elderly woman walked up behind him. He was curious as to why she seemed to be following and said, "May I help you?"

The old woman said, "I'm very sorry to be following you and hope I didn't annoy you, but you look just like my son who recently died. Would you mind if I went ahead of you?"

"Oh, no problem, sure go ahead. I'm in no rush you sure you don't need help?"

The old woman thought a bit and said, "Why yes there is something you could do. Would you say, 'Goodbye Mom' as I'm leaving? It makes me feel good."

"Sure," he said. As the old woman was leaving, he said, "Goodbye Mom!"

After he was done checking his items, he saw his total came to $247.25. "What! I only bought these few things?"

The clerk said, "Your mom told me you were going to pay for her groceries."

* An old man applied for a job as a Piano Player at a local nightclub. He was dirty and looked like a homeless person who hadn't had a meal in days. The manager nevertheless pointed to the piano in the corner and asked him to audition for the evening guests.

He played beautifully. All the patrons stopped talking and listened to the slow and beautiful melodious piano tune no one had ever heard before. After he finished, the crowd applauded loudly, and they cheered and begged for more music.

The manager said, "Wow! That was excellent! What do you call that wonderful romantic tune?"

"I wrote it myself. It's called, 'I'm Gonna Bang You for Hours Until You Can't Talk or Walk.'"

"Interesting," the manager said and hesitated, then he said, "Play one more tune for us?"

The old man agreed and played an upbeat tune that got everyone clapping. Most got up and started dancing. Those that weren't dancing were keeping time pounding their hands on the table in sync with the beat of the music. When he finished, the audience gave him a standing ovation and begged him to keep playing.

"You are fantastic!" the manager said. "What's the song called?"

"I call it, 'I'm Gonna Slide It into You Slicker Than Snot on Doorknob."

The manager paused and scratched his head. The old guy bent down to pick up a few dollars around his bench that missed the jar on the piano and the manager noticed his pants were split and he wasn't wearing underwear.

"Do you know the back of your pants are ripped and your underwear is gone?"

"Know it?" the old guy said. "Hell, I wrote it!"

* Joe was driving his old car down the street in an old neighborhood and smoke started to come out of the hood. Joe wasn't an expert mechanic, but

he was able to push his car to the side of the road, raise the hood and stared at the engine through the smoke.

Suddenly, he heard someone calling out in a rough husky voice, "I think there is a problem with the radiator. You need a new radiator."

Joe looked around and saw no one except a brown cat sitting lazily on a window. Then he heard the voice again, "I said it's the radiator, you need a new one!"

Joe looked at the cat and realized the cat that was talking to him. He stood there stunned, but the cat continued, "There's a service station down the street. They'll repair your car and get you a new radiator."

Just then, a little old lady called out from inside the house, "Kitty, Kitty Where the hell are you? Are you talking to people again?"

The cat suddenly vanished, and Joe walked up to the house. The little old lady said, "Yes? What is it?"

"My car...I've got engine trouble. You won't believe me, but just now a cat told me to change the car's radiator at the repair shop down the street. It's amazing!"

The little old lady nodded. "Yes, it is amazing. Kitty giving advice on cars. You probably wonder, what does Kitty know about a car? Well, don't listen to Kitty. The people in the repair shop down the street are cheats!"

* A very elderly grandmother finished shopping and was walking to her car in the parking lot when she noticed 4 young men getting into her car trying to drive it away.

For protection, the elderly lady carried a handgun and when she saw the young men stealing her car, she dropped her bags and pulled out her handgun and started screaming, "Get away from my car! I've got a gun!"

The four young men turned and looked at her and saw her gun, then jumped out of the car and ran like hell.

The incident so shook the elderly woman, she couldn't get her key into the ignition. She kept fumbling and fumbling with her keys and couldn't start the car.

As she calmed down, she noticed a soccer ball, a baseball cap, and two six packs of beer on the passenger seat next to her.

She got out and realized her car was parked 5 spaces down.

She went to the Police Station anyway and reported the incident to the desk sergeant who started laughing hysterically.

As the sergeant was trying to catch his breath, he pointed to 4 young men who had just come in to report a carjacking by a crazy old lady, who was waving a huge gun at them.

* Two little old ladies sat on a park bench to have their daily cigarette. One of them reached in her purse and pulled out a prophylactic.

"What's that for?"

"Oh, I use this condom to keep my cigarette dry, so it doesn't get wet."

The other looks puzzled then said, "Where did you get it?"

"At the drugstore."

The next day the other little old lady went into a pharmacy and purchased a box of condoms. The pharmacist asked her, "Are you sure these are the right kind of condoms you need?"

"Oh, it doesn't matter which kind, as long as they can fit over a camel."

* On his 60th birthday, a man decided to have a complete physical examination at a well-known clinic to get himself completely checked out.

After two days of tests, he met with the physician in charge who told him he was doing "fine" for his age.

Concerned about what "fine" meant, he asked the doctor, "Do you think I'll live to reach 85?"

The doctor replied, "Do you smoke cigarettes or fine cigars?"

"Nope." Said the man.

"Do you drink fine wines, excellent brandies, or any kind of alcohol?"

"No. I don't like alcohol." The man replied.

"Do you eat filet mignon steaks, fried chicken, bacon and cheese omelets, or barbequed ribs?"

"No, I avoid those foods." The man replied.

"Do you spend time in the sunshine, playing golf, or at the beach, or boating?"

"No, the sun bothers me," the man replied.

"Do you chase women, go to casinos, or the horse track?"

"No, I don't do any of that, hell, I haven't ever done any of that." The man said.

The doctor studied his charts, then looked at the man and said, "Then why do you give a shit if you live to be 85?"

* An elderly couple were walking through a park they hadn't been to in years and were reminiscing. The last time they walked through this park was at a time when they were in their twenties. There was no one around and strolled slowly as they reminisced.

As they walked, they came to a heavily bushed area where they had enjoyed sex when they were young. With devilish smiles, they decided to try it again and relive it.

The couple went into the bushes and began bonking standing up, then the husband speeded up and started bonking his wife furiously like a rabbit with its butt on fire! They were at it over thirty minutes, non-stop! Then they both fell to the ground completely exhausted.

"Bonkers!" She said. "You haven't given it to me like that in 40 years!"

"Forty years ago, there wasn't an electric fence in those bushes!"

* Be careful which party games you play. It would be very bad if you had a heart attack especially when playing charades."

- Demetri Martin

Shopping

* Joe was smoking in a convenient store and the counter girl told him, "Sorry, no smoking in the store, please."

Joe said, "Hey, why not? I bought this package of smokes here."

"Why? Well, we sell a lot of things in this store. Everything from prescriptions to prophylactics and just because we sell prophylactics, you can't start f*cking us!"

Sign Language

* A deaf-mute golfer walked up to the first hole to tee off. Suddenly, another huge golfer walked up and said, "Hey You Asshole! Nobody tees off ahead of Big Ray."

Being deaf the poor guy continued to prepare for his shot, so Big Ray knocked him down and kicked his ball off the tee. Big Ray then teed off and walked off down the fairway.

The deaf-mute got up, brushed himself off, teed up his ball and whacked it straight at Big Ray and hit him square in the ass. Big Ray doubled up in pain and fell to the ground. The deaf-mute walked by him and held up four fingers in Big Ray's face.

* Gross Humor. Joe was playing golf in Central America with a Costa Rican golfer. While putting on the 6th green a group of monkeys gathered on the edge to watch them putt.

Just as Joe was about to putt, a bug flew in his ear, and he pulled and poked at his ear to get it out.

Suddenly, the group of monkeys went crazy and jumped on the American and began beating him.

The monkeys ran off and Joe stood up in a daze, scratching his head completely puzzled about what just happened.

The Costa Rican golfer explained pulling your ear means, "F*ck You!" in monkey language. Joe was angry and vowed revenge.

The next day Joe purchased large knives, party hats, party horns, and a large sausage.

He put the sausage in his pants and took it all to the 6th green where the monkeys gathered again to watch him. He tossed several party hats, knives, and party horns to the monkeys, keeping one set for himself.

Knowing that monkeys mimic everything, Joe put the party hat on.

The monkeys looked at him, then put on their party hats.

Next, Joe picked up his horn and blew on it. The monkeys picked up their horns and did the same.

Joe grabbed his knife and the sausage in his pants and sliced it through.

The monkeys looked at the knives, looked at their crotches, looked at Joe, and pulled their ears.

* I don't like "yes-men" working for me. I see their sign language, their body language always showing submission and agreement. I want anyone who works for me to tell the truth period. Being honest and talking honestly is the most important thing an employee can do, even if it costs them their job.

- Samuel Goldwyn

Society in Decline

* Children now love luxury too much and have bad manners, and contempt for authority. They disrespect elders and love to talk instead of exercising.

- Socrates

* You wouldn't want democracy if you were able to read several long 10-minute interviews of average voters. After you read how they feel and what they know, you would look at other forms of government.

- Winston Churchill

* "We only learn from society. We are instructed well on what is happening. However, inspiration only arises when you are alone.

- Johann Wolfgang von Goethe

* Is it better to take action to prevent over-population, climate change, and other environmental disasters or do we let nature take charge and do it for us.

* Drugs: Caffeine Monday through Friday keeps us charged up and going well to make our constructive contributions to society. Alcohol from Friday to Monday keeps us stupid enough to prevent us from figuring out the disaster we are in.

- Bill Hicks

Stupidity

* It is totally okay to be stupid, or dumb, or funny, if that's what you like to do. It's best to be yourself rather than try to be someone else. If you try to be someone that another wants you to be, that's stupid, so just be yourself.

- Christina Grimmie

* Feeling stupid? Everyone feels stupid now and then. But the embarrassment from doing something stupid doesn't last if you think about all the others who did stupid things. Not taking yourself too seriously and laughing at your own stupid mistakes indicates a competent and confident person. Amazing stories of blunders follow in this section, and they make you wonder, "What were they thinking?"

* A man in California used his shotgun like a club to break his ex's car windshield. The gun discharged when he did it and he blew a hole in his gut.

* A mechanic in Alamo, Michigan trying to repair a truck, asked a friend to drive the truck at a high speed while he hung on underneath, so he could see what was causing an unknown noise. Everyone around told the mechanic not to try it.

But he did. He got his clothes caught and his friend found the mechanic wrapped around the driveshaft.

* An Ohio man walked into a police station with a wire sticking out of his forehead claiming someone had stolen his brain and he wanted to be x-rayed to prove it. He had apparently drilled a hole in his head looking for his brain and put a wire in to search for his brain.

* A North Carolina man awoke in the early morning by his bedside telephone ringing loudly. He inadvertently grabbed his handgun which he kept on his nightstand thinking it was his phone and the gun discharged when he put it to his head.

* A man in England received a notice in the mail that he was caught by a police camera speeding in his car and received a £40 fine along with a photo of his car. Instead of paying the fine, the man sent the police a photo of a £40 note. Police then sent the man a photo of handcuffs. The man paid the fine.

* Two blondes bought two horses and drove home with the two horses in a trailer and then put them in their stable.

"These horses are great! But this one is my favorite and from now on I'll be riding only this one." The first blonde said.

"My horse is fantastic too! So, from now on I'll always ride this one, said the second blonde.

"But how will we be able to tell the horses apart?" The first blonde said.

They thought about it and the second blonde said, "Let's cut off this one's tail."

The other blonde agreed, and the horse lost its tail.

The next morning, their friend, a brunette came by who couldn't figure out why one horse didn't have a tail? "Why did you cut off that one's tail? She asked.

The two blondes told the brunette they did it, so they could tell the horses apart.

The brunette said, "You two are idiots for cutting off the horse's tail! Can't you see the black one is a bit taller than the brown one?"

* A South Carolina prison inmate on a murder conviction spent several years waiting for his appeals to finish to avoid the electric chair. Finally, the last appellate court reduced his sentence to life in prison but while he was sitting on a metal toilet in his cell trying to fix a TV, he bit into a wire and fatally electrocuted himself.

* A New Jersey couple was injured when a one-quarter stick of dynamite blew up in their car at 2 am. They had been driving a long time and got bored, so they lit the dynamite "to see what would happen" and tried to toss it out the window. They later told police they didn't notice the car windows were closed when they tried to toss it.

* An Indiana man used a gas lighter to look down and check the barrel of a musket rifle that hadn't been firing well and was killed when the weapon discharged in his face as he accidentally ignited the powder of the loaded musket.

* Two young Canadian men both died in a head-on crash while playing a game of "Chicken" on their snowmobiles which resulted in a tie game.

* Another Canadian man fell to his death while he was cleaning his bird feeder on the balcony of his apartment on the 23rd floor. He had to stand on something to reach up to the birdfeeder and chose a wheelchair to stand on which moved while he was cleaning, and he went over the balcony.

* Two Alabama guys were injured badly when their pickup went off the road and hit a tree. This happened shortly after midnight. They were returning at night from a long trip of frog catching. The headlights on the truck were not working properly since the headlight fuse had burned out. They didn't have a spare fuse but one of the men found that his 22-caliber bullet would fit perfectly in the fuse box of the old pickup truck and got the headlights working.

But after going for a half an hour or so, the bullet discharged and struck one of the men in the balls. That's when the pickup left the road and struck the tree. The highway trooper was amazed the men admitted how this occurred.

When the wife of the man who was shot in the balls was informed of the accident, she inquired how many frogs did they get and if anyone had bothered to get the frogs out of the truck.

* Three men are sitting at a bar and the conversation turned to their wives and they started complaining.

The first one said, "My wife is so dumb, she carries the old keys to our house we demolished and remodeled last year, and we don't even have the same locks anymore!"

The second man says, "That's nothing, my wife is so dumb, she tries to listen to music on her phone, and she doesn't have any earphones!"

The third man says, "That's nothing, my wife is so dumb, she carries a purse full of condoms and she doesn't even have a dick!"

* An English man, Irishman and a Scotsman are sitting in a crowded pub.

The Englishman said, "The pubs in England are the best. You can buy one drink and get one free".

Everyone in the pub agreed and gave a big cheer.

The Scotsman said, "That's fine, but in my country, you buy one drink and get two more free drinks."

Again, the crowd in the pub gave a big cheer.

The Irishman said, "Ireland has the best pubs. In Ireland, you buy one drink, get another 3 drinks for free, and then they take you in a private room for a shag."

The Englishman says, "Wow! Did that happen to you?"

The Irishman replied, "No sir, it didn't happen to me. My sister told me that's what happened to her."

* "He who laughs last thinks slowest."

- Pinterest

* A ship goes down at sea and only two survived, a man and a small terrier who found themselves washed ashore on an island. The only other inhabitants of the island are a herd of sheep that graze on the lush grasses there.

Every day for a year the man scans the horizon for any sign of a rescue ship, and the little dog follows him constantly at his side.

Sitting by the fire one night the man resigned himself to spend the rest of his life on the island. He began running down the list of things he'll never be able to do again—have a burger and milkshake, read a book, take a hot shower, have sex…no more sex! He cries himself to sleep.

A couple of days later as he's watching the sheep grazing an idea pops into his head. Why, he could take one on for a partner, couldn't he? It would be despicable and disgusting to have his way with a sheep, but who would be around to witness it? Celibacy be damned!

The sheep are docile, and he easily corners one in a thicket in just a few minutes. He pulls his trousers down. The little dog begins frantically running in circles around his ankles, yapping and tugging at his trousers. He can't quiet the dog, so he gives up.

He tries again several times over the next few days, but the little dog's barking and tugging at his trousers stop him from it.

A few days later, he sees a ship in distress just off the coast. It sinks within an hour.

He's up early the next morning sifting through the debris that washed up when he spots an attractive woman grasping on a wooden mast and wrapped up in sails and rigging. She's unconscious and barely alive, but he rescues her and nurses her back to good health.

Days later, the man, the woman, and the little dog are sitting by the fire when the woman said, "You know, I never properly thanked you for saving my life. I'm willing to do anything to repay you, and I do mean anything."

The man's eyes widen. "Could you watch this little dog for me for about 10 minutes?"

* A blonde went to Walmart and was shopping pushing her cart down the aisle between shelves of merchandise which were stacked high. As she shopped, she saw a blue sweater through the merchandise she wanted to try on, but the sweater

was displayed in the next aisle. She couldn't figure out how to go to the next aisle.

She noticed another blonde walking in the next aisle and called out to her, "How do I get to the other side?"

The other blonde looked at her and said, "You're already on the other side."

* "It's dark in here isn't it?" One blonde said to the other blonde.

"I don't know; I can't see," said the other.

Tech

* I was a bit embarrassed," said Bill Gates. "Today, I couldn't help it, but I had some flatulence in an Apple store and almost blew out the doors. People got upset. Hey, if they had Windows, that could all have been avoided."

* Joe received a text message:

Sorry sir I am using your wife, day and night, when you are not at home. In fact, I use your wife much more than you do.

I am feeling guilty, and I hope you will accept my sincere apology.

Joe was stunned until a second message was received shortly thereafter:

I meant "wifi."

* Joe's wife sent him a text on a cold winter evening: "Windows frozen."

Joe sent a text back, "Pour warm water over them."

A short time later, Joe got another text from his wife, "the laptop is completely f*cked up now."

Too Many Lawsuits

* A man was having problems with his late model expensive car as he drove through a high crime area at 2 am on a Saturday night. As he drove, he found his brakes were going out and they eventually failed to work. He parked the car at the top of a hill and called a taxi and left his car on the street, planning to get a tow truck the next day to tow it in for repairs.

A car thief stole the car shortly thereafter and drove it downhill into a tree resulting in the thief breaking vertebrae in his back. The thief had a permanent injury and filed a lawsuit against the car owner.

The lawyer for the car owner asked the judge to dismiss the case arguing no one should profit by wrongdoing.

The thief's argument was that the car owner "should have known his car would be stolen" in a high crime area when he left it on the street at 2 am. He claimed all the car owner had to do was to leave a note on his car that it had no brakes.

The court held the thief had a valid case of negligence against the car owner for not reasonably foreseeing his car would be stolen and that someone would be injured trying to drive it away. He was therefore responsible if the thief could prove his allegations at trial.

Before the case went to trial, it was settled outside of court for an undisclosed sum.

UFC

* Ultimate Fighting Championship fighters do not have sex before a fight. The main reason is they don't like each other.

* I've got nothing against the guy except that he's kind of a piece of sh*t.

- Nick Diaz, UFC Welterweight

* When you lose, don't say anything or very little. When you win, say less.

- Matt Hughes, UFC

* "Not bad for an old man," said, Randy Couture years ago. He had retired from UFC fighting then he crazily decided to take on 6' 8" Tim Sylvia and wound up dominating the match and regained his Heavyweight UFC Championship.

Walked Into a Bar

* A dog walked into a bar and jumped up on the barstool and said, "Hi Bartender. Believe it or not, I am a talking dog. No ventriloquist, no voice throwing, this is me, the dog, talking to you."

"So what," the bartender replied.

"You're not impressed? Have you ever seen or heard of a talking dog before? Now I want a drink."

The bartender said, "You want a drink? Sure, just go through that door for the toilet."

* After several days crossing the hot Arizona desert, a cowboy staggered into a town as thirsty as

hell. He walked into the bar and was about to ask for a drink when a man dashed into the bar and yelled, "Big Joe is coming! Big Joe is coming!" Everyone in the bar jumped up out their seats and ran out of the bar.

The thirsty man still wanted his drink but when he looked around everyone had left so he walked behind the bar and poured himself a beer.

Just then he heard huge loud hoofs pounding away on the street outside. A huge man was riding a wild buffalo down the street. He stopped in front of the bar, tied the buffalo up. The ground shook as he stomped into the bar and tore the swinging doors off their hinges.

The huge man was the meanest and ugliest guy the cowboy had ever seen. The man slammed his fist on the bar cracking the top of the bar almost breaking the bar in half and said, "Give me whiskey! NOW!"

The cowboy grabbed a whiskey bottle and shakily began to pour a whiskey when the huge man grabbed the bottle and chugged all the whiskey down. Then he threw the empty bottle against the wall smashing it into a thousand pieces.

Then the gigantic man made a beeline toward the door.

The cowboy scratched his head and said, "You're leaving?"

The huge man turned around and said, "Hell yeah! Haven't you heard? Big Joe is coming! Big Joe is coming!"

Women

* If women ran every country, there would be no war, but some countries wouldn't talk to each other.

* One day Adam and Eve are walking around the garden of Eden when they see God down the road holding a case.

"Morning God," said Eve. "Whatcha got in the case?"

"These are two things left over from creation. I thought you both might be interested in either of these?"

God opens the case and says, "Okay, which one of you wants to pee standing up?"

"Me! Pick me. Pick me." Adam said. "I could just find a tree and pee standing up and I'd be able to do so much more in less time. C'mon, God, pick me, please."

"Well, okay," said God. Then God gave Adam the penis.

God looked in the case and said, "Okay, let's see what I've got left for Eve. Yes, here it is - multiple orgasms."

* "You may tell a joke or funny story which reaches someone's heart and inspire them, and who knows what they might do because of the laughs you bring them."

- Erin Morgenstern, The Night Circus

World

"If you want to make the world a better place, be trustworthy and respect people who are trustworthy.

"Be a friend and chose worthy friends.

"Don't tell a joke which might hurt someone. Don't laugh when someone else tells a joke that hurts someone.

"Being true to yourself is good for everyone around you since it gives them an example to be thoughtful as well. You will be loved for it and you will influence others."

- Russ Roberts, American Author, economist, and research fellow at Stanford University's Hoover Institution.

Thank you

Thank you for reading this book. We hope you enjoyed it.

If you liked the book, we would appreciate your giving us a brief review.

Team Golfwell

We Want to Hear From You

Thomas Edison, image from Creative Commons

"There usually is a way to do things better and there is opportunity when you find it."

- Thomas Edison

We love to hear your thoughts and suggestions on anything and please feel free to contact us at TeamGolfwell@gmail.com.

www.ingramcontent.com/pod-product-compliance
Lightning Source LLC
Chambersburg PA
CBHW021423070526
44577CB00001B/24